MW00657221

Why We Need Ordinary Language Philosophy

Why We Need Ordinary Language Philosophy

SANDRA LAUGIER

Translated by Daniela Ginsburg

THE UNIVERSITY OF CHICAGO PRESS   CHICAGO AND LONDON

SANDRA LAUGIER is professor of philosophy at University of Paris I Panthéon Sorbonne and a senior fellow of the Institut Universitaire de France. She is the author or editor of many books in French and several articles and chapters in English.

Originally published as Sandra Laugier, *Du réel à l'ordinaire:*
Quelle philosophie du langage aujourd'hui?
© Librairie Philosophique J. Vrin, 2000.
http://www.vrin.fr

The University of Chicago Press, Chicago 60637
The University of Chicago Press, Ltd., London
© 2013 by The University of Chicago
All rights reserved. Published 2013.
Printed in the United States of America

22 21 20 19 18 17 16 15 14 13   1 2 3 4 5

ISBN-13: 978-0-226-47054-2 (cloth)
ISBN-13: 978-0-226-03755-4 (e-book)

Cet ouvrage a bénéficié du soutien des Programmes d'aide à la publication de l'Institut Français. This work, published as part of a program of aid for publication, received support from the French Institute.

Ouvrage publié avec le soutien du Centre national du livre, ministère français chargé de la culture. This work is published with support from the National Center of the Book, French Ministry of Culture.

Library of Congress Cataloging-in-Publication Data

Laugier, Sandra.
   [Du réel à l'ordinaire. English]
   Why we need ordinary language philosophy / Sandra Laugier ; translated by Daniela Ginsburg.
     pages cm
   Includes bibliographical references and index.
   ISBN 978-0-226-47054-2 (cloth : alk. paper)—ISBN 978-0-226-03755-4 (e-book)
   1. Language and languages—Philosophy. 2. Realism. 3. Analysis (Philosophy).
   4. Philosophy, Modern—20th century.   I. Title.
P106.L3195813 2013
149'.94—dc23

2012043140

♾ This paper meets the requirements of ANSI/NISO Z39.48-1992 (Permanence of Paper).

Contents

Preface

Although analytic philosophy is beginning to be established in France, it suffers from a certain number of misunderstandings and prejudices. The latter are primarily the result of ignorance on the part of philosophers trained in a traditional practice of philosophy usually called—whether rightly or wrongly—"Continental philosophy," which in France is characterized essentially by the refusal of anything contemporary and/or not French in philosophy. Most often, French philosophy rejects analytic philosophy because its way of posing problems and its principal authors are not "canonical"—that is, they are not recognized by the philosophical institution. But fortunately, it must be said that such an attitude is becoming more rare, and analytic philosophy has little by little gained the right to be included in French universities, thanks in particular to the perseverance and pedagogy of several leaders. This new respectability is, however, at the source of a second level of prejudices and misunderstandings, on which I would like to shed some light here. Willingly positioning itself as a minority and even missionary force, analytic philosophy *à la française* has, quite understandably, tended to refuse the very diversity and plurality that give richness to its American model. It is often normative, even dogmatic—sometimes with regard to the rest of philosophy, but in fact most often internally, with regard to itself and its possible variations. Thus, French analytic philosophy can give the false impression that there is but one "conforming" and standard version of analytic philosophy. In addition, the establishment of analytic philosophy in France (because it was delayed) coincided, in reality, with the explosion of the analytic paradigm elsewhere in the world. It is this explosion that I would like to consider and account for in this book, by presenting certain current debates in order to draw some provisional conclusions regarding, in particular, the sense and possibility of a "philosophy of language" today.

Several reasons have guided my approach. In the United States, many philosophical trends have developed since the 1980s: the hardening of cognitivism, the rementalization of philosophy, the so-called postanalytic derivations, the return to the history of philosophy, the development of moral philosophy, and other such developments all weaken the idea of a single analytic philosophy or even method. But this multiplication of trends—each of which, it is amusing to note, has its French counterpart— is not necessarily the essential issue. The question is now rather whether in fact there is *one* analytic philosophy. The moment has come, it seems to me, both in the United States and in Europe, to investigate the very nature of analytic philosophy: its origins, its history, and its interpreta- tions of itself. Perhaps in this way it will be possible to better understand the stages of its development—especially, for what interests me here, (1) the gradual effacement of reflection on language and (2) the particular, rather marginal, place assigned to ordinary language philosophers such as Wittgenstein and Austin. We may also better perceive the specificities of the French reception of analytic philosophy, which—with a few brilliant exceptions—quickly turned to an analytic paradigm excluding ordinary language in order to move either toward a form of logicism or toward the philosophy of mind. The fact that Wittgenstein and Austin arouse sus- picion and sarcasm in the majority of analytic philosophers in France— reactions that are reinforced and even justified by the local success of a certain postmodern and consensus-based reading of Wittgenstein—dem- onstrates that a rather specific version of analytic philosophy has become dominant, not (or no longer) in the United States, but in France itself.

The background to my work of historical reinterpretation—which ob- viously is only sketched here—is a reflection on the status and very nature of America, which I pursue elsewhere. The tendency, out of ignorance or ideology, has long been to define American philosophy solely in relation to analytic philosophy; even the designation "postanalytic" philosophy, which we hear from time to time, remains within such a framework, while at the same time suggesting going beyond or rejecting the analytic heri- tage (such a suggestion is rather deceptive, because in order to go beyond analytic philosophy, it is still necessary to understand in what it consists). French-style analytic philosophy is most often dependent on this false rep- resentation that American analytic philosophy has for a long time given of itself, and the recent return to pragmatism is a typical example of this view. In reality, the history of American philosophy is complex in another way, and the establishment of logical positivism starting in the 1940s is but a recent and remarkable stage. It is just as remarkable that American philosophy in its institutionalized version rejected first what was most radical in the Vienna Circle's philosophy and then, during the 1960s, ordinary language philosophy. Against all expectations, this could lead us to bring these two philosophical currents—logical empiricism and ordinary language philosophy—together. This is one of the lines of interpretation I would like to follow here. What analytic philosophy in America and—in a more caricatural form—in France still has difficulty accepting is a certain antimetaphysical and antipsychological philosophical radicalness characteristic of its beginnings and perhaps effaced in certain of its later developments.

Thus, several prejudices are targeted here. First, the idea that analytic philosophy is American philosophy, but also the idea that American philosophy is analytic philosophy. Perhaps on account of the overly convenient and somewhat hollow term *Anglo-Saxon philosophy*, there is a tendency to define analytic philosophy as a sort of shared production of English and American philosophy, just as there is an attempt to define the history of American philosophy on the basis of analytic philosophy, which came to dominate it more than a half century ago. It is perhaps possible to investigate a twofold repression: by making analytic philosophy the very "nature" of American philosophy, the history of American philosophy is repressed—not only pragmatism, as is recognized today, but earlier traditions such as Emerson's transcendentalism. But the way in which American philosophy *became* analytic philosophy—for reasons that have less to do with its nature than with historical circumstances—is also repressed. Analytic philosophy as we know it is of recent constitution; it was born in the 1930s with the importation of the Vienna Circle's philosophy into American philosophy. What is most curious is that this transfer was achieved on the basis of an almost isolated incident: the meeting of Quine and Carnap in Europe in 1933; it was after this that the transfer of Viennese philosophy into America took place. Was this transfer as self-evident as the official history of analytic philosophy seems to say? How was American philosophy able to *inherit* this part of European philosophy? It is a matter here of the very definition of American philosophy, which is called into question as soon as one begins to look into its origins, and perhaps also of the very constitution of the analytic-Continental divide. Under the domination of analytic philosophy, we have become accustomed to thinking of it as "at home" in America, although it was born in Europe. It is as if American analytic philosophy had been set on repressing this moment of its history, the 1930s and the "immigrant" origins of its emblematic figures. Today, as this history is being rediscovered, the idea is emerging in the United States that "part of the task of discovering philosophy in America is discovering terms in which it is given to us to inherit the philosophy of Europe,"[1] as Cavell puts it. This does not mean going back to the analytic-Continental divide, or reducing it, but rather thinking within it and accounting for it.

We may think of Wittgenstein's reaction, reported by Waismann, to Schlick's decision in 1931 to teach in an American university—the hint of a process that would become general practice during the 1930s and 1940s: "What should be given to the Americans? Surely not our half-rotten culture. The Americans have no culture yet. From us, however, they have nothing to learn."[2] This remark came at a crucial moment when living philosophy was preparing to cross the Atlantic, with the installation of Vienna Circle philosophy in the American academic system. The fact that this integration took place at the cost of a transformation of the arguments of logical empiricism, strategically reinterpreted—notably in the direction of pragmatism, which was reanimated by the importation of neopositivist arguments—is a point that bears closer examination. This will not be my objective here, however.[3] With these few remarks, my aim is only to bring about a change in perspective. There is no sense in wanting to (re)import an American or analytic model to Europe, as if it were univocal and ahistorical. The time has come, on both sides of the Atlantic, to question the history that led from the "linguistic turn" to the current confusions over the philosophy of language itself and to its eventually being surpassed by the "philosophy of mind." Before proclaiming the end of philosophy of language—which would be quite convenient for all those in France who were never interested in it in the first place—it is perhaps necessary to examine the sense and aim of a philosophy of language. Such an interrogation has hardly been privileged in the French version of analytic philosophy (Jacques Bouveresse's *La parole malheureuse* is an exception). This is undoubtedly for the reasons I have already mentioned: an incapacity or refusal by most of the French representatives of analytic philosophy to call into question a paradigm that, first and foremost, had to be imposed or presented as unified, without taking into account the divisions that little by little appeared at the heart of American philosophy of language (for example, between two conceptions of the philosophy of language that we may broadly define as normative and descriptive). But perhaps it is also because analytic philosophy *à la française* is, as one American observer has aptly remarked, in the end, very *French*. It is French precisely in that it is exclusive, polemical, and easily scornful, as well as in the dominant choices that have gradually come out of it, which privilege certain areas of analytic thought, such as (for historical reasons) logicism or (more surprisingly, although ultimately understandable within the French context) metaphysics and, more recently, moral philosophy and the cognitivist version of the philosophy of mind. This is a rather particular phenomenon and one that certainly distinguishes France from America, where there is a greater variety of interests and centers of research, even though there is a dominant trend; but there is also, to a lesser degree, a difference from other European countries, where analytic philosophy is presented in a more varied way.

It is entirely normal and natural that a dominant paradigm—a "mainstream"—be formed in analytic philosophy, as elsewhere. What can be problematic is for a position or conversation to remain possible with respect to this mainstream—for the mainstream not to become conformist. Thus, I would like to allow a slightly different voice to be heard. It would lead to making visible once again a radical difference between the analytic path and the path of "classical" philosophy, a difference that, in my view, appears most clearly when one examines the methods of Wittgenstein and Austin. I find it interesting that today certain of the most creative American philosophers, following Stanley Cavell and Hilary Putnam, hope in this way to return to the origins of analytic thought. (I am thinking here of John McDowell, Cora Diamond, and James Conant, but there are many others, although they remain in the minority.) Beyond their differences, these philosophers would like, through the thought of Wittgenstein, Frege, or Austin, to rediscover a conception of, or rather a relation to, language that has gradually been lost in the scholasticism of analytic debates. The rediscovery is taking place in what can be called, following Cora Diamond, a "realistic spirit." Of course analytic philosophy has for decades been centered on the question of language's relation to reality, which has given rise to an entire classification of different sorts of realism, even antirealism and irrealism. But we will see that such a debate, despite its intrinsic interest, is more symptomatic than actually illuminating. The quest for or dogged claim to a "realist" philosophical position is in fact precisely what threatens to distance us from the real, as Austin already remarked at the beginning of *Sense and Sensibilia*—and as we may easily observe when we look at the controversies that have long troubled analytic philosophy. "I am *not*, then . . . going to maintain that we ought to be 'realists,' to embrace, that is, the doctrine that we *do* perceive material things (or objects). This doctrine would be no less scholastic and erroneous than its antithesis."[4]

My idea is thus that in order to find the real again, it is necessary to give up wanting to be "realist" in the philosophical sense or senses that have progressively been attached to this term, as well as wanting to define, ground, or justify a realist (or antirealist) attitude—and that it is this desire for or mythology of realism that distances us from the real. This may appear paradoxical. English has two terms, *realist* and *realistic*, to distinguish between two ways of understanding *réaliste*—one philosophical and the other ordinary (as, for example, in the expression "Be realistic . . . "). If it were possible to distinguish these two terms in French, it would be tempting to say that there is nothing realistic, in the ordinary sense, about the desire to be realist in the philosophical sense of the term or in the sense of definitions of realism, and more generally that what we are lacking in philosophy is not realism in the philosophical sense but in the ordinary sense. It is precisely this aspiration to be realistic in the ordinary sense, to recognize what is in front of us—at our feet, as it were—which we do not want to see, that we can discover in Austin and Wittgenstein. Such is the definition of the return to the ordinary that they advocate and which I will attempt to analyze and justify here. This has led me to examine the various presuppositions, principles, and methods of "ordinary language philosophy" and to discover in them a way out of certain present-day aporias of analytic philosophy. But at a deeper level, it seems to me that this "realistic spirit" we discover in Austin and Wittgenstein, which Cora Diamond has shown also has its source in Frege's logical thought and in the *Tractatus Logico-Philosophicus*, is the most radical thing analytic philosophy has to offer, and it is undoubtedly what analytic philosophy has the most difficulty accepting and (thus) making acceptable. Without going so far as to speak of forgetting or repression, as Cavell does with regard to Austin, we may wonder about how little interest ordinary language philosophy arouses today on both the American and the French sides. We may also suggest that on each side it is the antimetaphysical radicalness of the approach that consists in starting from ordinary language, as well as the *critical* novelty of Wittgenstein and Austin's investigations, that disturbs philosophers, whether they are settled in the comfort of traditional thematics or in the more recent certainties of the cognitive sciences.

As I attempt to show throughout this work, it is rather complicated to take analytic philosophy as a starting point for thought today, especially in France. One sometimes has the impression of being faced with a rather paralyzing alternative between imitation and divulgation. Thus, one either tries to integrate oneself into the current of analytic philosophy worldwide (by writing in English, participating in exchanges with the great American figures of analytic philosophy, and making one's little contribution to the debates under way). Or, one tries to spread analytic philosophy, to be a worthy representative of it, particularly in the face of other major philosophical currents (each of which also has its own standard version). Both of these positions have their merits, difficulties, and inconveniences. For the moment, the path of imitation has, with a few exceptions, yielded scarcely any significant results—so true is this that an American who is writing in English and who has been raised in the philosophical milieu is more likely to be original or innovative than a French convert is, no matter how talented the French philosopher. The path of divulgation, which is often quite useful, also scarcely allows one to avoid conformism, and it runs up against the obstacles already mentioned: the difficulty of even defining analytic philosophy, and the multiplicity of its tendencies. There would be little sense in wanting to propose yet another path, and it is not my intention to do so. Perhaps, however, it is possible to look for a new point of departure—by following the line traced by analytic philosophy up to now and by going back to Austin's method, for example: examining "what we would say when"; or to Wittgenstein's method, "Back to the rough ground!";[5] or to Frege's, where the exploration of logic and language allows us to escape metaphysics and psychology. In all these cases and in others, what we find at the end of the line is a *critical* will, all the more effective and radical in that it is not always expressed as such and sometimes takes on an ordinary and trivial appearance. These various expressions of a "realistic spirit"—in the ordinary and critical sense that I have defined—are what interest me here.

I would like to thank Jacques Bouveresse, Christiane Chauviré, Didier Deleule, Vincent Descombes, Michel Fichant, and Claude Imbert for their comments, criticism, and remarks, which were of great importance in editing this book, and for their encouragement in the pursuit of the project. A big thanks also to Jocelyn Benoist, whose help and support have been extremely precious to me, and to all my friends from the seminar "Le mental et le social." Finally, I would like to thank Alain Pernet for his assistance in finalizing the manuscript.

Introduction

The contemporary history of Anglo-American philosophy sometimes seems to be one and the same as the development of "analytic philosophy," which is most often presented as unified, coherent, and inevitable. But it is not certain that the very concept of analytic philosophy is so clear, nor, a fortiori, that a certain imposed version of this philosophy (or method) must have a monopoly over it. In France, analytic philosophy wallows in its presentation of itself as an oppressed minority. It is obvious that it took a long time for analytic philosophy to gain legitimacy in France and that its emergence today is due to years of patient work by a few pioneers (Gilles-Gaston Granger, Jacques Bouveresse, Pierre Jacob, and François Récanati, to mention only a few names). But now that analytic philosophy is present and active in the majority of French universities, it seems excessive to still want to see it as the stakes of a combat and for that reason to impose a facade of unity on it, in order to counter its (alleged) enemies. We may even wonder whether, lacking total hegemony, certain self-proclaimed representatives of analytic philosophy in Europe find the status of oppressed minority preferable to recognition within a pluralist framework. It would be interesting to rethink the reasons for the trend that, throughout the twentieth century, led analytic philosophy to construct itself in distinction to other currents. Whatever the case may be, it is perhaps time—following the example of its most inventive American representatives—to examine the very constitution of this philosophy: its history, stakes, and divisions.

Thus, I am going to try to show here the tensions inherent in the very definition of analytic philosophy. For some time now, numerous essays published in English have brought out the difficulties of determining the nature and origins of what is called analytic philosophy, which mainly

developed in the United States after the European immigration of the
1930s and 1940s. Because of these difficulties, it is appropriate to examine
analytic philosophy's starting point before thinking about any "postanalytic" philosophy. However, such a historical procedure would seem to be
incompatible with some of the established rules of what analytic philosophy became during a certain period, at least in the United States (and
sometimes still today in France). Analytic philosophy has long claimed to
be ahistoric, which amounts to the illusion of constant timeliness or new-
ness. As for myself, may I be permitted to claim a certain untimeliness
here. The problems that occupy me were discussed, in their first form, between 1950 and 1970 in the United States (Quine's *Word and Object* dates
from 1960), between 1950 and 1962 in Great Britain (the dates of publication of Austin's principal writings), and in 1958 even in France (at the
famous Colloque de Royaumont entitled "La philosophie analytique"),[1]
and they were greatly transformed and radicalized in the decades that followed, continuing through to the present. Thus they are at the origin of
many of today's debates—for example, the debate surrounding "realism."
The problems from the years between 1950 and 1970 frequently had their
origin in the difficulties of integrating concepts inherited from logical positivism into the dominantly pragmatist American context, beginning in the
1930s.

    This problematic origin is what makes the figure of W. V. Quine so
remarkable, especially because of his historical role in importing logical
empiricism and Carnap's work, to which he dedicated a series of lectures
(on Carnap's *The Logical Syntax of Language*) at Harvard University, as
early as 1934.[2] It is not by chance that Quine was both the one to bring this
inheritance to perfection and, after 1950, to "explode" its limits (see "The
Two Dogmas of Empiricism," 1951).[3] Elsewhere I have tried to show, in a
manner immanent to Quine's work, how his work was able to contain without contradiction both this empiricist heritage and the explosive (as the
entire subsequent history presented here shows) invention of conceptual
schemes and the indeterminacy of translation *and* of reference.[4] Since that
time, I have lost some of my scruples, without, however, giving up on seeing the coherence of Quine's work: it is clear that this coherence is maintained only at the price of irreducible tensions, irreducible to the point of
having provoked the present explosion of analytic philosophy as well as
certain relativist derivations sometimes called "postist" (for these, let me
make clear before specifying further, I have no sympathy; I distinguish
them sharply from the unique, but in no way "postanalytic," procedure

of Cavell, for example). It is my contention that one can extricate oneself from these philosophical difficulties not by fleeing ahead (for example toward cognitivism), but only by reflecting on the philosophical stakes represented by these difficulties. It seems clear to me now that it is not possible to hold together all the strands that can be extended from the work of Quine, Wittgenstein, and Austin: the critique of the myth of meaning, ontological relativity, robust or natural realism, the return to learning and to the ordinary use of language. And yet I am no less convinced that we must nevertheless try to do so (with full awareness of this impossibility), for it is exactly in the necessity and difficulty of making all this hold together that we can define the vitality and radicalness of the problematic we have inherited here. Let us attempt to define it further.

The problematic can, at first glance, be included within the framework of the *philosophy of language*. But then we would have to know what we are talking about when we use this term, which seems at once adequate and deceptive. All the work of the philosophers who interest me here, such as Quine and Austin, is constantly centered on an examination—an analysis—of language. But I will not be showing that the problems of philosophy are problems of language, or that they should be resolved, or even posed, in terms of a logical-linguistic analysis of language. There is nothing more boring than the philosophy of language when it speaks "only" of language. From this point of view, none of the philosophers with whom I am concerned here—neither Quine, nor Wittgenstein, nor Austin—do philosophy of language. The interest, but also the particular difficulty, of the definition and practice of the philosophy of language is that to talk about language is to talk about what it talks about (and how, and where). Austin expressed this very clearly in "A Plea for Excuses," in his own falsely superficial way: "One thing needs specially emphasizing to counter misunderstandings. When we examine what we should say when, what words we should use in what situations, we are looking again not *merely* at words . . . but also at the realities we use the words to talk about."[5]

Obviously this is not sufficient, and the following will, I hope, contribute to clarifying this declaration. But I believe that Austin stated the very stakes of a philosophy of language and of what is called the "linguistic turn." One of the central problems I am interested in here is precisely the nature of this "turn." It is characteristic that Rorty, in the preface to his anthology *The Linguistic Turn*, already commented with irony on this passage of Austin's, as if in so doing he was abandoning the final illusions about our knowledge of language's capacity to speak to us about the real:

for Rorty, philosophers after the linguistic turn renounce looking for the ways "we find out something about non-linguistic phenomena by knowing more about linguistic phenomena."[6] This criticism is inseparable from the idea, which has always been present in Rorty's work in one form or another, that a change of perspective like the linguistic turn should lead to a "dissolution" of traditional philosophical problems (32). It is clear that I do not share this point of view—first, because the "traditional" problems of philosophy are still alive and well, though undoubtedly in a specific form within the framework of my reflection here, and second, because in reality nothing is further from a thinker like Wittgenstein than the idea that difficulties in philosophy would disappear through something like the analysis or examination of language. This, in any case, is how I interpret him, and in particular his transition from the philosophy of the *Tractatus* to the *Investigations*. Whatever the case may be, a major question remains to be answered: Why are we interested in language, *Why Does Language Matter to Philosophy?* to make use of Ian Hacking's excellent title.[7] One of the answers I have tried to offer to this question in several of the chapters presented here is that the philosophy of language is concerned with what language speaks of: that is, the real. Thus, I share the perspective developed by Cora Diamond in her book *The Realistic Spirit*: the "realistic" spirit that, according to her, governs the philosophy of the first *and* second Wittgenstein is the renunciation of all mythology of an intermediary realm, external to language and to the world—whether this mythology takes the form of sense or non-sense, of meaning or the ineffable. This also explains why it is not *here* a matter of philosophy of language. Most of the time, philosophers of language concern themselves with examining meanings; as Hacking remarks, this is something that has become dominant in the philosophy of language—it could be called the "pure theory of meaning"—whereas one could instead, like the traditional empiricists (Hobbes, Locke, Hume, Mill), take an interest in language in order to pose philosophical problems—what Hacking calls "*applied* philosophy of language" and which according to him is at least as philosophically relevant as the "pure" theory. V. C. Chappell writes, in the introduction to his excellent anthology, that "what is new" in the twentieth century's particular form of preoccupation with language is not interest in language, which has existed since the time of the Greeks, but "the study of language in order to achieve results on other subjects—mind, morals, nature, even God."[8] Pure theory would then go in the direction of linguistics or semantics, whereas applied theory would remain for philosophy.

It is clear that, thus formulated, such a project is not without its own illusions, inherent—as the subsequent history shows—to the very project of philosophy of language in the twentieth century: in particular, regarding the real possibility of "obtaining results" or even any kind of clarification in all these domains of philosophy. What is of capital interest in Quine's work—this was the main point of my work on his "logical anthropology"—is the radicalness of the double criticism he makes: of meaning (of "The Myth of Meaning," originally, "*Le mythe de la signification*," which was the remarkable title of his lecture, in French, at Royaumont) and of analysis (the myth of discovering the categories of the "real" through an examination of language). Strictly speaking, Quine should bring about the renunciation, once and for all, of the project for a philosophy of language, whether pure or applied. This, by the way, is what leads certain of his interpreters and successors to advocate a new, mentalist or psychological, turn after the linguistic turn: since the analysis of language yields nothing satisfying, one might as well turn to the problems of the "mind." An essential part of my project will be to show that such a turn resolves nothing, and if it does not constitute a regression, it is at least, as Bouveresse has noted, something that has "done more to displace problems than to solve them"[9]—and thus that instead of renouncing the philosophy of language in favor of the philosophy of mind, we should step back a bit and attempt to understand the stakes of the linguistic turn.

The question is first and foremost realism. To keep, or return to, the project of an applied philosophy of language, but without the mythology of meaning, of reference, or of conceptual schemes—this is perhaps a way to redefine realism within the perspective opened by Wittgenstein in the *Blue Book* and in the *Philosophical Investigations*. Quine's radical theses on meaning led some to relativism or postism and others to naturalism or psychologism. I will refuse such an alternative; I will simply take Quine's "robust realism" seriously and apply what I have previously defined as his "semantic descent": to speak about language is to speak about the world, as his treatment of truth and "disquotation" shows. And this was indeed Quine's starting point (see the first words of *Word and Object*), even though he has little interest in usages, apart from linguistic usages. Thus, at the Colloque de Royaumont, he recognized an agreement in principle with Ryle and Austin, in spite of their obvious differences:

> I think one of the reasons why we prefer to concentrate on language is that if we turn directly to the problems of the foundations of reality we risk bringing in a

group of presuppositions that touch on the deepest conceptual schemes, on the most deeply rooted habits of thinking and feeling—in such a way that none of the discussants can oppose his point of view to those of others without seeming to commit a *petitio principii*. . . .

The utility of the approach that causes us to leave the conceptual level for the semantic and to concentrate on the manner of saying things instead of on things said, remains—even if one thinks, as I continue to, that the fundamental problems regarding conceptual schemes are of the same order as the fundamental problems of physical science or mathematic logic.[10]

Certainly there are fundamental differences, which will appear in what follows, between this understanding and Austin's, notably with regard to the ontological stakes of Quine's work. But Quine does indeed start from ordinary language, and from the ordinary in general: "The central and primordial function of language is to deal with common, standard-sized objects that we use familiarly—the kind found at market. . . . Words themselves are one species of such standard-sized common objects."[11]

Thus, we could define Quine's "logical point of view" on the basis of his integration of logic into the learning of everyday language.[12] But Quine's propositions would nevertheless remain unsatisfying—not conceptually, but with regard to his *description* of language: Austin, for his part, would never say that words are physical objects like others (primarily because for him "like others" doesn't mean anything). But what may be lacking in Quine's philosophy has nothing to do with the ritually decried insufficiencies of his behaviorism. Quine's behaviorism, like solipsism in Wittgenstein's sense, *means* something about language: to acquire it, we have nothing else at our disposition but what is given to us by others (the *majores homines* of whom Augustine speaks in the passage Wittgenstein cites at the beginning of the *Philosophical Investigations*) or the "sensory stimulations" Quine constantly invokes. In *L'anthropologie logique de Quine*, it was precisely this "social" dimension of learning language ("Language is a social art," to use Quine's slogan) that guided my examination of the status of logic and its integration into the conceptual scheme of knowledge.[13] It remained to delve into the nature of this community-based agreement on language, which Quine held to be "natural"—that is, interpretable in naturalist terms (which we find in the passages I have just cited): language, from everyday or infantile language to its most complex theoretical developments, is a product of evolution and is necessary to our "life"—keeping in mind that, as Quine sometimes says, man lives "by both bread and natural science" and that the necessities of our lives are more complex than we imagine.[14]

It is this naturalism, already quite specific in Quine, that I would like to redefine here. Several paths present themselves. First, starting from Quine himself: there is a tension between his skeptical theses (the indeterminacy of translation and of reference, and the critique of the myth of meaning) and his natural epistemology—a tension his commentators frequently point out. How can epistemology be grounded, even on itself, if the question of knowing what we are talking about (posed absolutely) is devoid of sense? An exploration of this tension leads to a new evaluation of the foundations of Quine's theory of knowledge and of the ambiguous or problematic nature of his realism. How can one advocate a "robust realism" while at the same time maintaining that this thesis is an assumption radically immanent to the "conceptual scheme" of science? This remarkable position of Quine's makes his philosophy the explosive center of all the difficulties inherent in the legacy of logical positivism. It is thus within an investigation of this legacy that the famous question—so widely discussed among Quine's successors today (notably Davidson and Putnam, not to mention, of course, Rorty and Searle)—of realism and antirealism must be asked.

Another question, after Quine, remains to be asked. The questions of realism and relativism came directly out of the constitution of the analytic philosophy paradigm, mainly by Quine, during the key period between 1940 and 1960. Quine was undoubtedly the first and last analytic philosopher who wanted to propose a *system* of philosophy, structured by interdependent theses and traversed, like all systems, by internal tensions—which are, by the way, what makes the system interesting. In this way, Quine brought the heritage of the Vienna Circle and empiricism to its naturalist version, grounded on or in the conceptual scheme of science, where truth and ontology are defined as immanent. This Quinean epistemology—called "naturalized" and so convincing that after it was proposed one wanted to naturalize anything and everything—can thus hardly be separated from his skeptical theses about the indeterminacy of translation and of reference; and one of its difficulties, which in my opinion has not yet been resolved, is the relation between what has become "standard" naturalism and the very particular form of realism Quine adopts. For me, one of the most interesting aspects of this naturalism (one that I have tried to bring out in this book) is the central role that the question of language learning, conceived not only in behaviorist terms but also in terms of community, takes in it. At first, the reflection on the *natural-ness* of language was simply posited as a common structuring element in Quine's and Wittgenstein's thought. But the question of language's naturalness subsequently became for me more of a difficulty than a passageway between Quine and Wittgenstein, as the thought of language learning in Wittgenstein has turned out to be more subtle than in Quine, despite multiple proximities, especially at the level of Wittgenstein's relation to behaviorism and linguistic "inheritance." To my mind, this difficulty can be understood only within a deeper examination of the question of *natural* language, henceforth the question of *ordinary* language. What is ordinary about the "natural," and inversely, in what way and in what sense is ordinary language natural (for isn't language also what is most conventional)? These are the problems that emerged, which we must now answer.

The idea was thus to pose not only the question of the *language of nature* (the relation, let us call it epistemological, between a theory of knowledge and the language of science) but also the question of *the nature of language* (the relation, let us call it logical, between the language of science and ordinary language). This made it necessary to reinvent another paradigm (to use, just provisionally, Thomas Kuhn's terminology) alongside the analytic paradigm that Quine both perfected and brought to its limit in pointing out its contradictions: the paradigm of ordinary language philosophy. One certainly has the impression that this paradigm has long since been abandoned, if it ever really existed. Here again the historical question of inheritance enters: the way in which logical positivism was inherited and reinterpreted in America excluded (even from the domain of linguistics) all examination of ordinary language for itself. It is obvious that a thinker like Carnap, who was, along with Quine, the founder of American analytic philosophy, played a determining role in the choice of an analytic paradigm (in the broad sense of an outcome of the project for a logical syntax of language) over a linguistic paradigm founded on an immanent examination of language. Here again, Quine seems to have resolved the matter: with the idea of the "regimentation" of ordinary language in logic, he extricated himself from the sophism of analysis (logic is not discovered in language but imposed on it, as is shown by his brilliant analysis, in "The Myth of Meaning"[15] and in *Word and Object*, of the translation of logical statements within the context of indeterminacy of translation). In this way he avoided the examination of language and its rules, which are always "projected" and reconstructed, even and especially in the case of a speaker's examination of his or her own language, "at home." This Quinean skepticism was taken to its limit by Davidson and his principle of charity. Thus, the question seemed settled: the rules of language's functioning, its logic as much as its ontology, depend on notation or on a choice of translation, or more generally on an interpretation, and there is no sense (or no "fact of the matter") in wanting to determine them. What hope is there for a philosophy of language and, a fortiori, for ordinary language philosophy?

This is precisely the context in which one can look anew at the theme of ordinary language philosophy. It is clear that the division carried out from 1940 to 1960 between the paradigms of the philosophy of language—between, on the one hand, the paradigm of logical clarification of ordinary language through an imposition of our rules, and, on the other hand, the much more fragile paradigm of an immanent examination of language through a discovery of its rules—seems definitive and that ordinary language philosophy today seems to have become obsolete. Two reasons make me think otherwise. Analytic philosophy, which for some time now has been focused on the debate between realism and relativism, does not seem to me to have gone any further than Quine, whether in developing the idea of immanent truth or in defending a realist position, and today it sometimes seems to consist in nothing but an inextricable scholastic debate—so-called postanalytic philosophy, represented emblematically by Rorty, which is both a vector and a symptom of the exhaustion of the analytic paradigm. It thus seems imaginable to take up the debate where it was artificially arrested in the 1960s, while at the same time taking into account what was achieved by Quine's philosophy: notably, his skepticism about meaning and ontology. Hilary Putnam, who has followed all the phases of the evolution of the analytic paradigm, thus invites us in his Dewey Lectures to invent a "second naivety,"[16] after the wars of position (particularly the debate over realism) that have been proper to American philosophy for several decades. Moreover, as recent works in the United States testify, it is time for us to reconsider the way in which the philosophy of the Vienna Circle was inherited in America, which then, paradoxically, impacted its reception in Europe—and one consequence of returning to the historical origins and course of analytic philosophy should be a reexamination of the place of ordinary language philosophy.

Contrary to what is often believed, the question of ordinary language and of the type of treatment it should undergo—normative clarification or internal examination—is present in and even constitutive of the heritage of logical positivism, as is testified by the work of Waismann (whose principal work, *Logik, Sprache, Philosophie* was published in English in 1965,[17] after having been composed in a different form in the 1930s) and, of course, by the work of Wittgenstein (the reception of which, within the American context I have just outlined, is highly problematic), each in its own way. Since Wittgenstein's work could not be integrated whole into the analytic paradigm, and because his relations with the Vienna Circle (whose most important representatives, fleeing Nazism, were the driving elements behind the construction of analytic philosophy in the United States) and also with America as such were rather difficult, it is clear that his influence must have worked on several levels. In analytic America the *Tractatus Logico-Philosophicus* is regarded with fearful respect, and it thus plays a role similar to the one it played in Europe in the 1920s. The work of the second Wittgenstein, apart from a few slogans ("meaning = use") cited without examination, was scarcely explored prior to Cavell's first works, in which Cavell maintained that "its reception is still to come." This is perhaps still the case today.

Wittgenstein obviously plays an essential role in this problematization, if only through the shift, in him and accomplished by him, from the first task of the philosophy of language I defined (to create an ideal or formal language to clarify everyday use) to the second task, which is to examine the multiplicity of the uses of common language, to look at our feet rather than above our heads. My goal is twofold and might seem contradictory: first, to demonstrate the radicalness of this change; nothing could be more false for me than Rorty's claim in his preface to *The Linguistic Turn* that "the only difference between Ideal Language Philosophers and Ordinary Language Philosophers is a disagreement about which language is Ideal."[18] In the renunciation of an ideal language or a norm exterior to language, there is a real change of philosophical perspective, consisting in abandoning the very idea of an ideal of language, of a beyond of language. This is what Wittgenstein, as early as the *Tractatus Logico-Philosophicus*, called "throwing away the ladder."[19] This leads me to my second goal, which is to demonstrate the antimetaphysical continuity of Wittgenstein's project, which, as Diamond and Bouveresse have shown, in a sense has always been the same.

What defines the continuity of Wittgenstein's project and thus, for me, is what is interesting in philosophy of language—and this will bring us back to Quine's project—is the search for a *logic* of, or in, language. For me, the shift from Wittgenstein's first to his second philosophy is not a change of method but an "extension" of the *Tractatus*'s method of analysis to ordinary language and to the question of ethics, aesthetics, or, in general, of our everyday judgments—which seemed to escape the domain of the analysis of language and meaning. We know that this extension is problematic and that it requires a change in the definition of analysis, as well as other more radical changes, and this is what I want to begin to elucidate. It is also to this end that I have turned to Austin: first, for his real and remarkable success in examining the elements of ordinary language (his brilliant text on excuses would suffice to testify to this),[20] and second, simply, for his philosophy itself, which has long been neglected (although it has been rediscovered in America, first under the impetus of Cavell and now that of Putnam). His is a philosophy that radically transforms the analytic paradigm and its conception of language and truth.

That, then, is a first glimpse at my project. To go from the real to ordinary language is neither a renunciation nor even a transfer. Two possible misunderstandings of such a statement would indeed be possible: one could interpret it either as the affirmation that it is necessary to abandon the exigencies of scientific discourse and knowledge (the standards of rationality, as some would say) in order to "shift" to ordinary language, or as the project (sometimes discussed in Austin) of a veritable science of language, which would give us knowledge of our language on the same grounds as natural science. In what follows, I will attempt to avoid these misunderstandings. Wittgenstein's work, like Austin's, shows that from formal to ordinary language our goal or "need" (which can be described as "logical") is the same. As Wittgenstein says:

> We see that what we call "sentence" and "language" has not the formal unity that I imagined, but is the family of structures more or less related to one another.—But what becomes of logic now? Its rigour seems to be giving way here.—But in that case doesn't logic altogether disappear?—For how can it lose its rigour? Of course not by our bargaining any of its rigour out of it.—The *preconceived idea* of crystalline purity can only be removed by turning our whole examination round. (One might say: the axis of reference of our examination must be rotated, but about the fixed point of our real need.)[21]

My goal is thus to show that the rigor required in the examination of the rules of ordinary language is equal to that required in logic (this is what I have tried to do with regard to Austin in particular) and that this rigor poses problems comparable to those raised by the constitution of logic in Wittgenstein or, precisely, in Quine. As for the second misunderstanding, it seems clear to me that it is based on a common philosophical conception, exactly the one my argument will try to reverse: that science (and philosophy, in certain of its dreams) is built by going beyond language and our ordinary uses of it: as if one would start from ordinary language in order to arrive, through clarifications and rectifications, at the language of science and the real. On this point, ordinary language philosophy goes against the whole philosophical tradition (whether Platonic, idealist, or empiricist) as much as or more than against the arguments of logical positivism. I wish to reverse this conception of ordinary language (which obviously has been given great credibility in philosophy) in order to demonstrate the problematic nature of the relation between ordinary and scientific language within science itself, as well as to suggest the complexity of ordinary usages: the fact that there is, so to speak, nothing ordinary about ordinary language (that it is out of the ordinary, if one may say so); that the disquiet summed up in the question *Must We Mean What We Say?* to quote Cavell's title, is everywhere in it. Beyond his reading of Wittgenstein and Austin, all of Cavell's work is focused on demonstrating this point.

Obviously, such a project of going from the real to the ordinary via the routes of logic (*From a Logical Point of View*, to use Quine's title) is not free of paradoxes and pitfalls. In order to undo the analytic paradigm, it is necessary to rethink logic, to depsychologize psychology, but also—and why not—to "demoralize" morality without naturalizing them; to conceive the naturalness of language without naturalization and to rethink language philosophically, outside of the field of philosophy of language: these are ideas that, although they seem paradoxical, nevertheless outline a project. One could call this project, once again and for the last time, realist—even if it is a matter of a radically new realism that has nothing to do with "realism" as it has been defined, developed, and dissipated by analytic scholasticism. Realism here is neither a thesis nor a position in the great conversation of philosophers, which sometimes deafens us to the point of preventing us from hearing "the voices of ordinary language." And realism is no more a thesis in the first Wittgenstein, when he writes in the *Remarks on the Foundations of Mathematics*, "not empiricism and yet realism in philosophy, that is the hardest thing."[22] To be realist without being empiricist, but without forgetting why one wanted to be empiricist. This very particular form of realism, which guides the second philosophy of Wittgenstein and which Cora Diamond presented in *The Realistic Spirit*, is what I would like to bring out in my interpretation of the philosophy of language.

It is clear that all this necessitates a rereading of the recent history of philosophy, at least on American shores. This will indeed be the method used: to reconsider the history of analytic philosophy and the very status of history within this philosophy, which amounts to giving back a place to currents like ordinary language philosophy, which, although they were not dominant, nevertheless marked the evolution of this philosophy from underground and in the long term. This brings us to consider, as always, the question of origins and heritages. There are several ways to cast doubt on the official history of analytic philosophy: by giving importance to the "linguistic" current (this is the goal of my return to the debates of the 1960s over the "linguistic turn," notably those between Cavell, Katz and Fodor, and Rorty); by insisting on the European origins of American philosophy (through two parallel cases, Carnap's presence in Quine's work and thus in all of analytic philosophy, which was born in America out of the emigration of the Vienna Circle, and the considerable influence of Pierre Duhem and Emile Meyerson, little known in France, on American epistemology between 1950 and 1960); or by rediscovering, inversely, Emerson's influence on the European nineteenth century, repressed along with America's transcendentalist past. It is in a sense a rereading of the history of American philosophy and its relations to Europe that I am proposing as a program here (a rereading that obviously remains to be completed and for which I have only placed a few markers and made a few hypotheses, just in order to shake up an overly idealized or fixed image), in order to open up new areas of research.

This history is certainly more complex than is believed. Only relatively recently has "scientific" analytic philosophy begun to be represented as having distanced itself from all concern with ordinary language and usage: it is clear, when one looks back to the period I am interested in here, between 1950 and 1960, and to the texts typical of this moment that ordinary language philosophy—or linguistic philosophy, the expression typical at the time—is a continuation of logical empiricism and at the same time a critique of it, and that it preserves its guiding principles: for example, the rejection of psychologism or rather (since it is not simply a matter of "antipsychologism") the invention of a "nonpsychological" point of view (see the *Tractatus Logico-Philosophicus*),[23] or the project of *describing* ordinary language through its *rules*. If evidence of this were needed, the complex and contradictory work of Waismann, who went from being a member of the Vienna Circle and a meticulous student of Wittgenstein to Oxford and "linguistic philosophy," would testify to it, as would Austin's itinerary and of course the passage from the "first" to the "second" Wittgenstein, which I interpret as continuity. This continuity has recently been reaffirmed by Diamond, Bouveresse, and Conant, and one may discover the arguments for it in Cavell's first texts, "Must We Mean What We Say?" and "The Availability of Wittgenstein's Later Philosophy," which date from 1958 and 1962, respectively. Here again, it is by going back to this crucial period in the philosophy of language (around 1960) that we can glimpse both the connection between ordinary language philosophers and their analytic predecessors and the sense of the break that seems, a posteriori, to have established itself between the two currents. Undoubtedly this was due, as can be shown,[24] to the establishment of a certain dominant institutional model of analytic philosophy in America, the repercussions of which we are feeling in France, belatedly as always. The current difficulties in the reception in France of Cavell's work—which is, however, recognized in the United States—recall the debates in America during the 1960s and the rejection by Fodor, who has since become the pope of cognitive sciences, of ordinary language philosophy beginning in 1962. The same is true of the desire on the part of certain analytic philosophers to implement a single dominant paradigm of analytic philosophy today in Europe, whereas in the United States its explosion is now a simple reality—one that can either be deplored, out of nostalgia for a conquering, univocal, and self-confident analytic philosophy, or celebrated, as Putnam and Cavell do, in the hope of a new starting point (a second chance) for the philosophy of language.

CHAPTER ONE

From Empiricism to Realism

We may begin by comparing three different "stagings" of language. The first (in nonchronological order) is well known,[1] Quine's scene of radical translation: the linguist in the jungle studying an unknown language accompanied by a native who cries "gavagai" when a rabbit runs out in front of them. The second is the scene invented by Wittgenstein in §2 of the *Philosophical Investigations*, based on Augustine's description in the *Confessions* of learning language, a description Wittgenstein cites at the beginning of the *Investigations*. There is a mason A and his assistant B, and their language consists entirely of the words *block, pillar, slab*, and *beam*. A pronounces, calls out these words, and B brings the object "which he has learnt to bring at that call." The third scene, which will be addressed later, is from Austin, and with it begins *How to Do Things with Words* (there are, in fact, several scenes: the "I do" pronounced in response to the priest's question in a wedding; the "I name this ship the *Queen Elizabeth*"); this scene differs from the first two if only in that it takes place within a social and institutional context. Without having changed fundamentally, my interest has shifted from the first, Quinean scene of radical translation to the plurality of Austinian scenes by way of a specific interpretation of the first scene—an interpretation authorized by the second, Wittgenstein's critique. The three points of view presented here share in common a criticism, stated in different ways, of the myth of meaning. It remains to be seen what this expression means, and this issue has turned out to be more complex in Quine than one might have expected. Quine's goal is to critique, and his thesis of indeterminacy is essentially negative. But it is still necessary to determine exactly what he criticizes and what he means by *myth*. This term, which occurs frequently in Quine's work, points to what is at stake in his philosophy: the *anthropological* critique of the myth of meaning as the myth of a core common to different languages, as the reintroduction of a universal of thought or language that one would have supposed the very process of analysis had eliminated. This critique is thus simultaneously an *epistemological* critique of the myth of meaning as a myth of reference or denotation, as a myth of a shared ontology common to different physical theories or conceptual schemes.

Clearly, these two critiques and these two myths overlap; they are, Quine says, "at root identical." I have sought to determine the relations and hierarchy between the theses of the indeterminacy of translation, the inscrutability of reference, and ontological relativity, by showing how Quine always proceeded by several paths—proving the first thesis on the basis of the second or the third, the third on the basis of the first, and so on, thus constituting a veritable system. It then became apparent that the inscrutability of reference—which became, importantly, the indeterminacy of reference after *Pursuit of Truth*—was the central point. It was not that the problem of reference replaced or supplanted the problem of meaning, but that the question of the myth of meaning—and the anthropological problem it raised—was already the question of language's relation to the world, and of realism.

We know that Quine first proposed the expression "myth of meaning" in 1958 at the Royaumont conference,[2] even though the problematic appears in several earlier texts (for example, "The Problem of Meaning in Linguistics," republished in *From a Logical Point of View*). This is because from the beginning Quine gauged the provocative aspect of the problem, which can be summarized in five points.

1. As is clear from the Royaumont conference, Quine's thesis targets the idea of a core common to different languages and the idea of an intermediary entity that would guarantee equivalence or correspondence between them. "What I take issue with, in particular, is the idea of an identity or community of meaning under signs, or a theory of meaning that makes meaning into a sort of supralinguistic abstraction, of which the forms of language would be the counterpart or expression."[3] This is precisely the Fregean idea of meaning (*Sinn*) as a core common to languages, which constitute its "shell" or expression.[4]

2. Quine's thesis is an anthropological one. First, it raises the problem of interpretation in anthropology and in the domain of the human sciences as a whole (as Descombes has suggested). My goal in critiquing Davidson's, or Davidsonian, theories of interpretation has been to restore the original skepticism of Quine's thesis. There is nothing "to be right or wrong about," as Quine said, and thus no *reason* to always interpret a

foreign utterance in what would be the most reasonable (for us) manner. Of course, the radicality of Davidson's skepticism must not be underestimated either—but what I would like to question is a certain use of Davidson to trivialize the principle of charity and make it a principle of the universalization of rationality.

3. The thesis of the indeterminacy of translation bears on the indeterminacy of reference. It presents an ontological problem, although it is not based on any concern for ontological economy. "Hume, not Occam, is my inspiration." This reminder of Quine's, made at Royaumont, should be remembered by all those who consistently approach the thesis of indeterminacy from the standpoint of "Occam's razor, Plato's beard." The ontological problem of the thesis of indeterminacy is, in fact, the impossibility, or rather inanity, of asking the native, the other, but also myself "what one is talking about." From this point of view, (anthropological) indeterminacy has inevitable consequences at the epistemological level, though not exactly as one would expect—it raises the question, among others, of what the objects of a/the theory of physics are. In one sense, it seems that if we follow Quine to the end, there is no answer to this question.

4. The thesis of indeterminacy does not counter mentalism (even if it *could*). It is true that in "The Problem of Meaning in Linguistics" Quine states that "the idea of an idea, the idea of a mental counterpart of linguistic form, is worse than worthless for linguistic science. I think the behaviorists are right in holding that talk of ideas is bad business even for psychology"[5] (he was thus rejecting, one might say, psychologism even in psychology). But this is not the problem. In "Ontological Relativity" Quine specifies that "the naturalist's primary objection to this view is not an objection to meanings on account of their being mental entities, though that could be objection enough."[6] From there to saying that the thesis of indeterminacy is compatible with a restored or even minimal mentalism is a step I refuse to take. It seems to me even less possible to find in Quine a reintroduction of mentalism or psychologism via an examination of the radical interpreter's "attributions of beliefs."

5. The thesis of the indeterminacy of translation bears on the ordinary use of language. This is the point that today seems most worthy of examination. At first glance, the thesis can be expressed in terms of the problem of the synonymy of statements or terms. Why isn't the thesis of indeterminacy an ontological thesis? "Readers have supposed that my complaint is ontological; it is not. If in general I could make satisfactory sense of declaring two expressions to be synonymous, I would be more than pleased to recognize an abstract object as their common meaning. The method

is familiar: I would define the meaning of the expression as the set of its synonyms. Where the trouble lies, rather, is in the two-place predicate of synonymy itself; it is too desperately wanting in clarity and perspicuity."[7] In an important article, "Use and Its Place in Meaning," Quine takes up Wittgenstein's question from the beginning of the *Blue Book*: "For a provisional solution, consider what we often actually do when asked the meaning of a word: we define the word by equating it to some more familiar word or phrase. . . . We may persist, then, in the old routine of giving meanings by citing synonyms."[8] This takes us back to the very definition of the "myth of meaning," an expression, let us recall, that comes from Wittgenstein: "Negation: a 'mental activity.' Negate something and observe what you are doing.—Do you perhaps inwardly shake your head? And if you do—is this process more deserving of our interest than, say, that of writing a sign of negation in a sentence? Do you now know the *essence* of negation?" In a note to this passage, Wittgenstein comments, "The fact that three negatives yield a negative again must already be contained in the single negative that I am using now. (The temptation to invent a myth of 'meaning.')"[9]

If, as Wittgenstein says, we are "tempted" to invent a myth of meaning, it is for good reason; we know how important the voice of temptation is in Wittgenstein, and it is not necessarily to be resisted, but rather simply to be heard and understood. Despite all his denials of a "fact of the matter" of translation, Quine never says that statements "don't mean anything." They "signify" or rather mean, *in the ordinary sense*. In "The Myth of Meaning," Quine asserted at the outset: "It is not my intention to demonstrate that language presents no meaning. I do not disagree that the words and phrases we use have meaning, in the ordinary sense of "have meaning.""[10] For Quine, it is better to think of the verb "mean" as intransitive: statements mean, but this is not to say that they mean or signify some thing, a meaning. Thus, in "Use and Its Place in Meaning," Quine proposes beginning with "mean" as an intransitive verb: "An expression means; meaning is what it does, or what some expressions do. To say that two expressions are alike in meaning, then, is to say that they mean alike. Some expressions sound alike, some mean alike. It is significant that when we ask for the meaning of an expression we are content to be given another expression on a par with the first, similar to it in meaning. We do not ask for something that the two of them mean. The French idiom is more to the point: *cela veut dire*." One may posit objects that are meant in common by statements that "mean alike" (rather than mean "the same thing").

For once we understand what it is for expressions to mean alike, it is easy and convenient to invoke some special objects arbitrarily and *let* them be meant....

... If we can manage this, then we can blithely say thereafter that expressions that mean alike *have* the *same meaning*.[11]

The problem is that we do not know what it is "to mean alike"; nor—in particular, since the expression is more common—do we understand "to mean the same thing." The empirical criteria Quine proposes in *Word and Object* collapse by themselves. This is the very object of his thesis of indeterminacy: there are no empirical or behavioral criteria for the synonymy of expressions or terms. Quine pursues the work of destruction begun in "Two Dogmas of Empiricism," claiming that there is no empirical meaning, not only (from the point of view of holism) because one cannot distinguish the empirical content of an isolated statement, but also for a supplementary reason, one that thus subordinates the epistemological to the logical in Quine's philosophy and unifies the double criticism found in "Two Dogmas." This is the impossibility of correlating two statements in two different languages, or, more precisely, the fundamental indeterminacy and arbitrary nature of any kind of correlation. The thesis of indeterminacy and the assertion that meaning is a myth "contaminated" Quine's entire system, to such an extent that they then spread to all of analytic philosophy's discussions and determined the very terms of the debate between realism and relativism.

It is clear that a part of this debate stems from Quine's rejection of meaning. However, Quine does not reject meaning, or rather, the "to mean." Instead, his goal, given the absence of a "fact of the matter" of translation is to render meaning intransitive—the *cela veut dire*. There are no entities that are meant by language; there is only language. For Quine this does not mean that, as Rorty would say, we have lost the world, for it is only in language that it is to be found. "Truth is immanent."

It is now time to explore the sense of these claims Quine makes. My orientation is radically opposed to any theory of interpretation inspired by Davidson and to any relativism à la Rorty. (The two are not as different as one might think, and, paradoxically, they join each other at a certain level). One might think that in the absence of a "fact of the matter" of translation, in the absence of meaning or an intermediary *Sinn*, all that we are left with is the theory of interpretation, the play of conceptual schemes and the communality of language. But it seems to me that Quine means just the opposite. It is now no longer a problem of interpreting, adequately or not, Quine's work and theses. A new problem has been raised by his successors and their endless discussions of realism, which are only now beginning to exhaust themselves. Quine poses the question of realism, but he resolves it immediately—he thinks—by affirming an "immanent truth."[12] I would like to show that he does in fact resolve the matter, but in a way that has not been understood (this lack of understanding was inevitable, and it led to the debate over realism) and could not be understood within the framework of his work alone, which wants to affirm empiricism and realism at the same time. This misunderstanding has been shared by Quine's successors and critics Davidson, Putnam, and Rorty, each in his own way. It is my belief that in order to understand what realism consists in, or what the "realist spirit" is, we must stop putting the question of realism into the framework of empiricism. This would amount to undoing the connection between empiricism and realism that seems fundamental in the work of Quine and others. But, does realism in Quine's work depend on empiricism? I am always brought back to Wittgenstein's affirmation that the most difficult thing is to have "not empiricism, and yet realism."[13] To determine the sense and stakes of this, it is useful to return to the empiricism-realism connection in Quine. As an examination of Quine's relation to Carnap's work would show, there is, despite everything (and in spite of the great coherence of his work), a tension in Quine between two tendencies. There is the naturalist or (although it is not the same thing) pragmatist tendency proclaimed in the famous last lines of "Two Dogmas," and there is the conventionalist or "linguistic" tendency in the style of Carnap. It is true that, after "Truth by Convention" (1935), and even as early as his 1934 lectures on Carnap, all the way down to his most recent works, Quine never stopped criticizing the doctrine of "truth by convention." But he criticized it less in order to give up on this doctrine than to give content to conventions—in a sense, to justify them. This was Quine's initial project, formulated in a text from 1937, "Is Logic a Matter of Words?": to empirically reconstruct logic. "Such a reconstruction would lend substance to the linguistic doctrine of logic—and would seem, incidentally, to merge with the empiricist's program of delineating the connections of all statements with direct observation."[14] Such a project, as hopeless as it may seem, contains the seed of Quine's entire work and all its contradictions, along with today's tensions within analytic philosophy. It is a matter of preserving the rigor of the laws of logic while connecting them to experience. "A principal virtue of the doctrine [that logic is wholly a matter of linguistic decision] is the clarity with which it explains the a priori character of logic," Quine writes in this piece.[15] But if logic is a matter of language—and Quine has always said that it is, in the trivial sense—it is not therefore a matter of convention (except in the trivial sense in which anything that has to do with language is conventional), not *mere* convention. This is because every convention has its reasons—natural reasons, as Cavell says in a different context[16]—and also because logic, inscribed within language, within the conceptual scheme, is no more or less connected to experience than the scheme taken as a whole. As Skorupski has noted, convention is not a matter of choice: "It is not that we 'agree' on a 'convention.' Rather, we discover that we share in common a certain constraint or limit in our thinking. The 'limits of empiricism' are not *conventions*. They are ways in which we naturally go on."[17]

The influence of Carnap may explain the tension between empiricism and conventionalism in Quine's work. Quine says he is an unswerving empiricist, and he proclaims this empiricism anew in response to Davidson's lucid criticism of "the very idea of a conceptual scheme."[18] For Quine it all begins—to use his favorite expressions, which he continued to use through to his most recent works—with our "nerve endings" and other stimuli and "surface irritations." This typically Quinean vocabulary should not make us forget where all this ends: in the constituted conceptual scheme—that is to say, in language, our language, which speaks of objects. It is Quine's very empiricism that inaugurates the distance—the underdetermination—between our ("surface") data and our objects, from the most ordinary to the most refined. And it is this empiricism that gives rise to the seemingly "relativist" or, in any case, instrumentalist remarks on the "myth of objects" in the "Two Dogmas": "As an empiricist I continue to think of the conceptual scheme of science as a tool, ultimately, for predicting future experience in the light of past experience. Physical objects are conceptually imported into the situation as convenient intermediaries—not by definition in terms of experience, but simply as irreducible posits comparable, epistemologically, to the gods of Homer. . . . The myth of physical objects is epistemologically superior to most in that it has proved more efficacious than other myths as a device for working a manageable structure into the flux of experience."[19]

I cite this passage almost in its entirety in order to show how all the discussions, epistemological or generally philosophical, which have since troubled analytic philosophy can be drawn from the "Two Dogmas." The question of realism—the question of the reality of the entities postulated by theories to account for experience, and of the irreducibility of these entities (posits) to sensorial data—is at the very starting point of Quine's philosophy. This initial observation concerning the irreducibility of such entities to sensorial data simply belongs to the given of philosophy and is part of our Humeian heritage ("Hume, where we all belong"): we have nothing but our experience, which gives us neither knowledge nor objects. Quine never goes on to question this observation; instead, it is radicalized by the very thesis of the indeterminacy of translation, which unexpectedly acquires (contrary to certain of Quine's claims) epistemological validity.[20] Thus, objects will be "posits" and our ontology will be "relativized" to the choice of a background theory. The counterpart to this ontological relativization is the myth of objects and the indeterminacy of reference. Once this relativity has been admitted, it remains to save, so to speak, realism. On the one hand, one may reaffirm realism in a manner immanent to science and to conceptual schemes—"truth is immanent, and there is nothing above it." Putnam has for years now made a sport of denouncing this form of realism as nothing more than empty words.[21] It nevertheless remains the case that Quine's position here has exceptional strength and has inspired more than one form of realism as well as antirealism—many present forms of realism being nothing but refined forms of antirealism (Putnam, who mocks the teratology of realisms, gives some of the best examples of this). On the other hand, a second solution would find a different form of realism—not a realism "by default," "nevertheless," or even "robust," nor a return to hard-core, preanalytic realism. Cora Diamond's "realistic spirit" is a notable example of this second solution, but in large part the way remains to be found. The choice is not so simple, and if there does indeed exist a "natural" form of realism that is not simply the other side of ontological relativism, it can be found in part in Quine's naturalism. This is because in spite of everything, it is in Quine's insistence on the use, inheritance, and learning of language—in what I have called elsewhere his "philosophy of immanence"—that the first indications of another form of realism can be discovered, one inherent to our common use of language. There is, however, a price to be paid for this realism: the renunciation of empiricism, or rather, of a certain form of empiricism that makes us expect knowledge to come from our "nerve endings" and consequently to affirm, fatally, that the real, which thus cannot be given to me, must be "posited" or invented. "Not empiricism, and yet realism."

CHAPTER TWO

Relativity, Conceptual Schemes, and Theories

Quine's thesis of indeterminacy is inseparable from his empirical point of departure, although it is distinct from his affirmation, in "Two Dogmas of Empiricism," of the underdetermination of theories by experience. However, this distinction, which Quine makes explicit several times, is attenuated by certain consequences of indeterminacy and ontological relativity. The thesis of the indeterminacy of translation also bears, unexpectedly, on the ontology of science and thus on epistemology.[1] Thus, the simple underdetermination of theories by experience becomes in Quine a radical thesis, a relativization of science's object and the very notion of *fact of the matter*. In fact, it would have been enough to adhere to the letter of Quine's first texts in order to realize this and to see in his mature works not a renunciation of but an addition to these first arguments. When Quine maintains that the "myth of physical objects" is a cultural production intended "for working a manageable structure into the flux of experience,"[2] he is simply stating, in different form, the relativist or rather immanentist thesis of "The Problem of Meaning in Linguistics," the third chapter of *From a Logical Point of View* and the first formulation of the thesis of indeterminacy: to draw conclusions about the ontology of a native language is to project our own ontology onto it. "The lexicographer comes to depend increasingly on a projection of himself, with his Indo-European *Weltanschauung*, into the sandals of his Kalaba informant." As Quine famously put it, there is then no "fact of the matter" of translation; "There is nothing to be right or wrong about" (63). This point, which Quine already raised in *From a Logical Point of View*, determines the continuation of his philosophical trajectory in its anthropological as well as its ontological consequences. Indeed, it is necessary to take into account the extreme coherence of this book, Quine's first and undoubtedly most radical philosophical work, which at first glance appears to be no more than a collection of articles. In analytic secondary literature we are so used to reading collections of separate essays brought together more or less artificially in one volume that we fail to see the systematic unity of *From a Logical Point of View*, which connects the ontological theme ("On What There Is") to an epistemological criticism ("Two Dogmas") and to the thesis of the indeterminacy of translation ("The Problem of Meaning") in order to produce a theory of the "myth of objects" and of "conceptual schemes." In a sense, Davidson hit the mark when he called his target, the "very idea of a conceptual scheme," the source of all discussions on realism and empiricism. The idea of a conceptual scheme presented in every chapter of *From a Logical Point of View* is in fact a war machine against a certain form of realism—the empiricist form, as it were: realism as "dogma of empiricism," as the thesis of individual adequacy of our statements to fragments of the world. Quine does away with the idea of empirical content as well as with analyticity, and he thus seems to renounce realism: all ontology is relative, as he already stated in "On What There Is" (19), well before "Ontological Relativity." And this is nothing to worry about. The question of language's adequacy to the world is "spurious" (a word we will find again in Austin), as Quine quite logically concludes in the fourth chapter, "Identity, Ostension, and Hypothesis." The question emerges from language itself, and we can answer it only if we "talk about the world as well as about language, and to talk about the world we must already impose upon the world some conceptual scheme peculiar to our own special language" (78). This means that the question of realism is in any case immanent. Davidson's error thus lies not in his criticism of the idea of a conceptual scheme, which is particularly perspicacious, but in his solution. Certainly one cannot but agree with his proposal to do away with scheme-content dualism and with his project to "re-establish unmediated touch with the familiar objects";[3] and certainly the idea of a scheme applied to a raw given, slicing it up into manageable pieces, is a considerable step toward idealism or, as Davidson says, relativism. But one cannot give up this idea without understanding why and how it was arrived at, nor can one reject it alone while retaining the rest of empiricism's approach and all of analytic philosophy as it was constructed in America on the basis of Carnap and Quine. Incidentally, Davidson recognizes this at one point but does not draw out all the consequences: the "dualism of scheme and content, of organizing system and something waiting to be organized, cannot be made intelligible and defensible. It is itself a dogma of empiricism, the third dogma. The third, and perhaps the last, for if we give it up *it is not clear that there is anything distinctive left to call empiricism*" (189). If we take Davidson's philosophy of language seriously, it is necessary to give up empiricism. Why not? But it is equally necessary to give up the philosophy of language—the idea that language speaks of "something." It is not certain that Davidson's theory makes it possible to take this step, nor is it certain—as Putnam has reminded us in all his recent writings— that there is any sense in wishing to do so. All of American philosophy of language is based on this famous third dogma, which is simply its rule of interpretation of empiricism: we have "only" experience, and from it we must produce knowledge, invent language, construct our theories. What a miracle—how do we do it? This is a recurring theme in Quine and is a constant in all post-Quinean philosophy.

From this point of view, Davidson's criticism seems to me necessary at a certain level. Davidson truly saw a difficulty in the anthropological position that can be derived from Quine's arguments. This difficulty is not relativism, as Clifford Geertz has very convincingly demonstrated in his fascinating text "Anti Anti-Relativism": relativism is essentially an invention of antirelativists, intended to promote their "pasteurized" form of rationalism.[4] Nor is it exactly the "very idea of a conceptual scheme"—the idea of a formless given cut up with concepts that are incommensurable with it (for this idea of a brute given is not present in any of the theoreticians Davidson targets; it is found perhaps only in Whorf). The problem is in fact the very idea of something given in experience to be translated into language, the idea that language itself is developed on the basis of experience. But what can one oppose to this?

Let us turn again to Davidson's approach. In the passage quoted above, Davidson wants to include his approach within the tradition of the "two dogmas," while from the outset criticizing their insufficiency. Quine certainly rejected synonymy and meaning, but he did not finish off the other dogma—linked to reductionism—although he maintained it was identical to the first dogma, analyticity (they are, he said, "at root identical"). Thus, Quine, in rejecting the dogma of the analytic-synthetic distinction, introduced in its place the idea of empirical content, a given (what in Quine is often called "surface irritations" and "sensory stimulations," to quote his hardly attractive vocabulary)—certainly an indeterminate and inseparable given, but nonetheless present. As we know, Quine was the first to deny the existence of *individual* empirical content of statements. Contrary to what Davidson says, this did not lead him to endorse the idea of a global "content" to be organized. For Quine, the real is not a formless given that would be "organized" or carved up by language; it is defined internally to language. To quote Putnam's joke, Quine does not believe in "immaculate perception."[5] Clearly this is a problematic position. The difficulty, as we shall see, lies not in the idea that there is a given, but rather in the idea that we "fabricate" or weave our knowledge and statements out of this given ("man-made fabric" is Quine's famous expression in "Two Dogmas," where he represents knowledge as a fabric of statements). Once there is such a "fabric," there is indeterminacy and a plurality of schemes and interpretations, as Quine first and most radically showed. Obviously, one can be tempted to make a further reduction and say, like Davidson, that there is no longer anything but these interpretations. But it is clear now that Davidson's solution (even if it leads him to present a form—certainly highly sophisticated—of realism) displaces the question by a *petitio principii* instead of resolving it. It is not enough to say that there is only language and objects, with nothing "in between," even if Davidson's theory of semantics, by reconstituting meaning on the basis of Alfred Tarski's theory of truth, has tried to substantiate this argument. The theory of interpretation, especially as taken up by Dennett and by Davidson's disciples, has to the contrary—and contrary to Davidson's initial "monist" project—led to a return of meaning in a form just as mythical as the one criticized by Quine: for example, in the form of cognitivists' intentionality or, more generally, in the idea of attributions of belief. Thus, the initial radicalism of Davidson's argument, like that of many of Quine's, has been weakened by various interpretations and argumentations in which it has played an official role. The initial argument—the refusal of an intermediary elaboration between language and the world, and its presupposition, the refusal of the myth of meaning—has thus been forgotten. Only the argument's naturalism has been retained, and a new myth has been invented, the theory of interpretation. The idea of a third dogma is strong, and it shows the direction in which to look for realism, but in the form in which this idea has spread, it hardly brings us closer to "re-establishing unmediated touch with the familiar objects whose antics make our sentences and opinions true or false."[6] To cite a theme dear to Davidson, this project is now of the order of "wishful thinking."

It is perhaps by examining more closely Quine's claim to a "robust" realism, linked to his empiricism, that one can better understand the unsatisfactory character of the Davidsonian solution and the forms of realism produced by post-Quinean scholasticism. This is because, in spite of everything, Davidson's remarks in "The Very Idea of a Conceptual Scheme" point to a difficulty in Quine's realism—even if they are also a radicalization of several incidental remarks from Quine's "first philosophy." Let us return for a moment to *From a Logical Point of View*. In the chapters following "Two Dogmas" and "The Problem of Meaning in Linguistics"— in particular, "Logic and the Reification of Universals," "Notes on the Theory of Reference," and "Meaning and Existential Influence"—Quine implacably pursues his definition of a conceptual scheme. He begins by presenting his first version of what would later become ontological relativity. "I am not suggesting a dependence of being on language." This does not mean that being is independent of language, but rather that there is no sense in asking whether it is or not. For Quine, our task is entirely different. "What there is does not in general depend on one's use of language, but what one says there is does."[7] In *L'anthropologie logique de Quine*, I examined the work thus assigned to philosophy and the establishment of the "logical point of view," and I will not dwell on this here. What is of interest in Quine's ontological theses lies in their apparent triviality: what exists is everything, *every*thing. But, Quine remarks in his first personal philosophical intervention at the beginning of "On What There Is," this certainly does not efface all possibility of disagreement on what exists, on what a thing is (1). To say that what exists is every*thing* is thus to observe both an obvious fact and a radical indeterminacy. Hence the famous Quinean criterion, now at the point of becoming as paradigmatic as Russell's definite description, that "to be is to be the value of a variable," becomes a triviality. As Harman said, "His criterion is the truism according to which what a theory says exists is what a theory says exists; once the canonical notation is adopted, his theory becomes a truism."[8] The first step toward relativism is this apparent modesty of the task Quine defines. Ontology does not have to determine what is. "What is under consideration is not the ontological state of affairs, but the ontological commitments of a discourse."[9] Quine stated this limitation in "On What There Is": "We look to bound variables in connection with ontology not in order to know what there is, but in order to know what a given remark or doctrine, ours or somebody else's *says* there is; and this much is quite properly a problem involving language. But what there is is another question" (15–16). From here to saying Quine supports a form of critical realism that supposes the existence of an independent but unknowable real, there is but a step.

Before taking this step, however, we must examine another point of view often put forth by Quine: science tells us what there is, and there is nothing beyond it. He could have said, parodying a sentence of Wittgenstein's, that "it is science which tells us what sort of object a thing is." This conception does not fail to raise serious difficulties as soon as one begins to examine what, in fact, the objects of science are. There are always several ontologies possible to account for a single empirical given. This is the most remarkable thing Quine established in his "late" philosophy, and it is very clearly summarized in the first chapter of *Theories and Things*. From this point of view, the indeterminacy of reference also plays a role in the epistemological domain, despite Quine's denials, and there is no more a *fact of the matter* in the choice of a physical theory (between two empirically equivalent theories) than there is in the choice of a translation manual.

In reality, this indeterminacy is due to Quine's conception of ontology. Ontology is normative, and its function is not to make the existential assumptions of our ordinary discourse appear—just as the job of canonical notation is not, Quine repeats, to explain all of ordinary language's turns of phrase. Quine is thus very far from the idea of an ontology implicit in ordinary language, but this is because he also rejects the project of determining the ontology of the language of science. And this, in turn, is because in any case the objects of science are for Quine inscribed within a continuation of our ordinary objects, which signifies less the naturalness of these objects than the theoretical nature of *all* objects, including ordinary ones (again, see the essay "Theories and Things"), and, in general, the continuity between common objects, "those found at market,"[10] and the more specific and indeterminate objects of science. The most theoretical objects are constituted on the basis of primordial physical objects, which we learn to refer to when we learn language. "Bodies are the prime reality, the objects par excellence. Ontology, when it comes, is a generalization of somatology."[11] As for the abstract objects of philosophy, they are imitations or generalizations based on the "prototypical objects" of ordinary language, just as objects like "molecule" or "electron" are constituted on the model of primordial bodies (like "mama," "dog," etc.). There is continuity, as Karl Popper also said in his own way, between the roughly individuated bodies from the beginning of linguistic learning and the more sophisticated objects of science and philosophy. Inversely, our everyday objects are theoretical—they are "posits." "All objects are theoretical. Even our primordial objects, bodies, are already theoretical."[12] The very notion of an object finds itself challenged by theoretical indeterminacy, and before Davidson it was Quine who involuntarily began to call into question the idea of a nonobjectival given: in spite of his talk of sensorial reception and stimuli, Quine indeed seems to say that we can only speak of, and think in, objects. Our ontology is immanent to language. But by affirming at the same time that this objectival scheme, which he also calls the "myth of objects," is a cultural production applied effectively to the "flux of experience," Quine gives rise precisely to "the idea of a conceptual scheme" and to the indeterminacy of reference. It remains to be seen whether one can really avoid this indeterminacy and along with it "the idea of a conceptual scheme," while at the same time preserving the immanence to language.

Indeterminacy is the direct result of the Quinean conception of "formalism" or canonical notation. The essential philosophical merit of this conception was to do away with the idea of unveiling the ontology of language or science and to weaken the idea of a "natural ontology"—even before this came into its current form, notably within cognitivism. Canonical notation no more "unveils" ontology in language than it reveals an underlying grammatical structure within it. As Quine says in *Theories and Things*, "Putting our house in ontological order is not a matter of making an already implicit ontology explicit by sorting and dusting up ordinary language."[13] Thus, we realize that there is no sense in wanting to determine the ontology of a scientific theory. This obviously agrees with Duhem's conception of the ontology of physical theories, which in this respect is remarkably close to more recent problematics. The ontology of a theory is as undetermined as the ontology of a native language in radical translation, and this is indeed because in Quine, just as in Duhem, theory *translates* experience—in an indeterminate translation. This empties the ontological question when posed in general. "What makes ontological questions meaningless when taken absolutely is not universality but circularity."[14] The ontology of a theory can be determined only within the framework of another theory, called the "background theory." I have shown that in this way there is in Quine a double, even a triple relativization of ontological questions: first, one cannot ask what exists, only what a theory says exists. Next, one can ask only what a theory says exists relative to a background theory; and finally, one can ask only what a theory says exists relative to the necessarily indeterminate translation of the "object" theory into the background theory. In this way Quine invents a dedramatized form of relativism. Of course reality is immanent: even the notion of "fact of the matter"—which is so often invoked to argue for Quine's initial physicalism and to distinguish in spite of everything theoretical underde-termination from the indeterminacy of translation—is itself immanent. "What counts as fact of the matter" can change. "Factuality, like gravita-tion and electric charge, is internal to our theory of nature." Of course, ontology depends on language. Of course, truth is immanent.[15] We always speak from within a theory, just as radical translation indeed shows that we always speak within our language. There is no *pou sto*. To recognize the indeterminacy of language is to recognize the arbitrary nature of our "objectifications"—in radical translation, the arbitrariness of "reading" our conceptual apparatus in a native language; in physical theory, the ar-bitrariness of the ontological problem of the nature of science's objects. In each case there is indeterminacy: for in each case, the object is "pro-jected" and constructed—never discovered. Indeterminacy is linked to the "logical point of view" and to the status of formal notation. In reality, the "conceptual scheme" is the notational scheme, and we must continue to place the question of the status of logic at the center of Quine's philo-sophical system. What we may at present call into question, after having examined all the consequences of such a conception of logic, is the very idea of language's "regimentation" in canonical notation. Certainly such an idea is preferable and less mythical than the idea of "discovering" the structures of language and mind in logic—an idea with which Quine had definitively finished (and "good riddance," as he himself said regarding a certain form of empiricism) (39). This is probably the only understanding of logic actually acceptable after the thesis of indeterminacy. But never-theless there remains a problem: realism. Quine's thesis made possible all the "postanalytic" claims about the uselessness of positing the real once we have language or languages; no need for the world, as Rorty would say. Language is enough, and then some. In his second preface to *The Linguistic Turn*, "Twenty-Five Years After," Rorty renounces the entire procedure of his 1967 anthology and the project of discovering something in philosophy through examining language. He takes up the Davidsonian criticism of "the idea of a conceptual scheme," interpreting it rather ju-diciously as an ultimate consequence of Quine's criticism of representa-tionalism. According to Rorty, Quine and Davidson showed us that we do not need to examine language in order to discover anything about reality. Rorty cites Davidson ("A Nice Derangement of Epitaphs," another fasci-nating text by Davidson):[16] "We have erased the boundary between know-ing a language and knowing our way around in the world in general."[17] Worlds, words: the identity between the two, stated by Davidson, becomes

in Rorty an argument for the uselessness or end of the philosophy of language. "There is no such thing as a language," says Davidson—not if we
understand by language "anything like what many philosophers and lin-
guists have supposed": a means of representing and communicating the
real. Language, says Rorty, is no longer representation, but only a social
practice, a means "used by human beings in the development and pursuit of social practices." We must "[give] up the idea of 'a language' as a
structured medium of representation, capable of standing in determinate
relations to a distinct entity called 'the world'" (373–74). My question,
then, would be this: in renouncing language as representation, as Quine
and Davidson do, and in renouncing a univocal relation between language
and the world, is it necessary also to give up on language? Rorty adds in his
1992 postface that "the basic idea of linguistic philosophy as [he] defined it
in 1965—the idea that philosophy could be advanced by studying a topic
called 'language' or 'our language'—was deeply flawed, deeply implicated
in a *non*-naturalistic picture of human knowledge and inquiry" (374). I
am not so sure of this, even if Quine, after Wittgenstein, was right to do
away with language as representation, and even if Davidson was right,
also after Wittgenstein, to be done with the "given" as object of language.
There is a way *after* Quine and Davidson to think language, and not only
as some great universal cultural conversation. To give up representation is
not to give up the "saying" of language. Indeed, it seems to me that Rorty
and Davidson have not perceived all the stakes of the philosophy of language beyond which they attempt to go. This is, first, because Rorty's and
Davidson's renunciations of the philosophy of language have—despite
Davidson's denials—led to a sophisticated form of relativism, referred to
as immanent, "quasi," or internal in Putnam or Blackburn. Second, it is
because we have not yet finished with the idea of philosophy of language
as an examination of language's capacity or claim to speak the real. From
this point of view, it seems to me, if not amusing, at least symptomatic
that the end of the philosophy of language (often associated with the end
of philosophy "in the traditional sense," whatever that might mean), is
announced both by followers of Rortyian relativism and by advocates of
cognitivism and the philosophy of mind, self-proclaimed heralds of anti-
relativism. Whether one seeks to go beyond the philosophy of language via
cultural relativism or a new mentalist turn, what is forgotten (repressed,
Cavell would say) is language as it was first put forward to philosophy: not
as something made, but as simply "given," already there.

CHAPTER THREE

Truth, Language, and Immanence

Indeed, Quine here again opens the way for us. What, in fact, is the meaning of his "robust realism"? For Quine, the ontological question, which is indeterminate or inscrutable in the case of translation and even "at home," can be arrested within the framework of our language. "And in practice we end the regress of background languages, in discussions of reference, by acquiescing in our mother tongue and taking its words at face value." Ontological discussions come to an end on their own (as Wittgenstein says, "explanations come to an end somewhere"), through "uncritical acceptance," as Quine says,[1] of the uses of words we have learned. It is learning that makes agreement possible—nothing mental is posited here. This led me, in *L'anthropologie logique de Quine*, where my analysis was based precisely on the idea of learning, to insist on the internal obviousness of ordinary usages—which is, however, the result of a learning that takes place through radically indeterminate means. As Quine always said, translation begins at home, and my neighbor's ontology is as inscrutable to me as that of the most distant indigene: it is just that the learning we share with our neighbors does not ordinarily result in asking the ontological question; that question emerges only in situations of radical translation. Such is, once again, the anthropological sense of radical translation and of the question of language. "Even we who grew up together and learned English at the same knee, or adjacent ones, talk alike for no other reason than that society coached us. . . . We have been beaten into an outward conformity to an outward standard; and thus it is that when I correlate your sentences with mine by the simple rule of phonetic correspondence, I find that the public circumstances of your affirmations and denials agree pretty well with those of my own" (5).

One could thus establish a parallel between the terms *parochial* (provincial, small-town) and *inscrutable*, which constitute a fundamental structure in Quine's work. Our objectival scheme is parochial, but it becomes inscrutable if we want to examine it from the outside. In short, "parochial" and "inscrutable" are two sides of a single point of view. This obviously leads to viewing Quine's realism with a skeptical eye, if it is immanent or parochial in this way. It is indeed from the parochial point of view that Quine states his realism—how else? He concludes "Speaking of Objects" thus: "In saying this I philosophize from the vantage point only of our own provincial conceptual scheme and scientific epoch, true; but I know no better."[2]

Quine's affirmation of realism, always reiterated in his work, has meaning only provincially, just as his refusal of relativism does. "Have we now so far lowered our sights as to settle for a relativistic doctrine of truth—rating the statements of each theory as true for that theory, and brooking no higher criticism? Not so. . . . Within our own total evolving doctrine, we can judge truth as earnestly and absolutely as can be; subject to correction, but that goes without saying."[3]

Did Quine, as Paul Gochet has recently said, really succeed in reconciling empiricism and realism?[4] It is not so certain. Indeed, it is not possible to really believe in his "robust realism" once one is aware of the indeterminacy of reference. But what does "robust" mean, anyway? Let us return to the passage from *Theories and Things* where the expression appears for the first time: for Quine, the conceptual scheme and "the scientific system, ontology and all, is a conceptual bridge of our own making," and nevertheless he firmly believes "in external things—people, nerve endings, sticks, stones" and, "less firmly, in atoms and electrons and classes. Now how is all this robust realism to be reconciled with the barren scene that I have just been depicting?"[5] As we can observe here, *robust* is a term with a complicated usage in Quine; it is a qualifier that today we would tend to call "thick." "Robust" is not just a factual qualification of the solidity of his relativist thesis but indicates its status as a thesis, as a claim (an affirmation made "nevertheless")—made even if the question of its justification is problematic. My purpose here is not to indulge in an excessively detailed analysis of Quinean usages but to get a sense of what is claimed with the word "robust": a mixture of obligation ("one must indeed") and obstinacy ("in spite of everything"), which makes it less a qualifier than a signal. As the text then goes on to indicate, it is the signal of an often-obligatory reference: naturalism. "The answer is naturalism: the recognition that it is within science itself, and not in some prior philosophy, that reality is to be identified and described."[6] Realism is "robust" because it is immanent to our language and to our acceptance of science and because it does not need to be justified once we are within the framework of a naturalized epistemology. Thus, Quine instituted a certain use of "robust" and more generally a form of naturalism within American philosophy. Any thesis one does not try to justify other than through naturalism—that is to say, by referral to the functioning of knowledge itself—is robust. Of course, Hume had established the naturalist approach by appealing to habit, custom, and human nature in general in order to justify certain of our inferences; Quine took this up, maintaining in "Epistemology Naturalized" that our knowledge and conceptual scheme do not need some first justification and that there is no sense in looking for one, once they constitute satisfying means of prediction and conceptualization. It remains to be seen whether this process of naturalization can be reiterated with regard to themes like realism. The process is perfectly argued in the case of our belief in the resemblance of the future to the past, and it can be extended to the entirety of knowledge once, in Quine's case, knowledge is also defined as an instrument of survival in the broad sense he gives to the term. For Quine, this is perfectly coherent, since his realism is immanent and in a sense trivial; in other cases, however, realism or other theses are, with reference to Quine, considered to be "naturally" justified. One may observe that this becomes a problem and that many of the references to the natural as "robust" are forms of begging the question, as Hume himself would say. What, in fact, is naturalism?

Contemporary naturalism, notably in the form in which it has become a cognitivist *argument*, often has little naturalism left in it—at any rate, none of Hume's problematic and skeptical naturalism—since it consists in wanting to ground and justify positions in an alleged human nature, which is redefined ad hoc. Quine's move, like Hume's, was to trivialize the question of justification: to "justify" knowledge by knowledge, science by science. It is not certain that we can go beyond this point and justify anything "through science" other than science itself. It even seems at first glance that this would be something quite different from naturalism, even its opposite! Whether one wants to naturalize morality, intentionality, rationality, or, as in this case, realism, the illusion (or dogmatism) remains the same: to have both naturalization and foundation at once.

It was clearly Quine who, in spite of explicitly limiting his own naturalism to the field of epistemology, opened the way for the scientistic version of naturalism: by including ontology within the extension of the work of science, he could indeed have seemed to want to justify "naturally" a certain ontology and thus a form of realism. However, the question of realism is trivial or lacking in content for Quine. The content we give to the word *reality* is produced by scientific discourse and is integrated into an "immanent epistemology." It is this immanent epistemology that in *Theories and Things* "evaporates the transcendental question of the reality of the external world."[7] It does not replace ontology but rather renders the question of realism—posed in general, or externally—futile. Internally, however, it seems as if there is in Quine a justification of realism other than through naturalism: a justification through the use of language, which is of sufficient interest for me to insist on it.

One could say that in Quine realism is part of the usage of the language of science. If we follow his naturalism, realism is in fact nothing other than the auto-affirmation of science. This self-affirming capacity is furthermore proper to ordinary language and to the language of science, which in Quine is always an extension of ordinary language. Here we may think of Quine's analysis of Tarski and Davidson's reprise of it. It is sometimes puzzling to observe the almost offhand way Quine treats Tarski's definition and limits its philosophical and definitional scope. The essential importance of the truth predicate is to "make us take words as they are" (as when one decides to take the terms of ordinary language at "face value" and not ask the ontological question). For Quine, there is no nontrivial definition of truth, and this is how he interprets Tarski's "Convention T." The passage to metalanguage and the appeal to the predicate of truth are only "tricks." The function of the truth predicate is not to assign a "value" (truth) to statements. It has a "cancellatory" function and does not define a quality—truth—of a statement. "This cancellatory force of the truth predicate is explicit in Tarski's paradigm: 'Snow is white' is true if and only if snow is white. Quotation marks make all the difference between talking about words and talking about snow."[8] For Quine, the truth predicate is simply a way of erasing the quotation marks, of "disquoting." To say that a statement is true is to reaffirm that statement. "In speaking of the truth of a given sentence there is only indirection; we do better simply to say the sentence and so speak not about language but about the world" (11). This recalls what is known as the "redundancy theory" of truth, as Frank P. Ramsey and Wittgenstein defended it: to say that a statement is true is to assert the statement. For Quine, although this is clearly contestable, the difference between this theory and Tarski's semantic theory is not so great. Of course, the "redundancy theory" was a sort of trivialization of truth. But Quine considers that there is no reason to fear this trivialization. This is what he means by the affirmation "truth is immanent." In the same way,

Tarski's definition as reread by Quine shows that knowing whether "snow is white" is true is the same as knowing whether snow is white. The answer is in knowledge, not in language. Science tells us what is, and it constitutes the only general answer to the question of truth.

Using the truth predicate is thus a means of talking about the real and is only in appearance a "metalanguage." "The truth predicate serves, as it were, to point through the sentence to the reality; it serves as a reminder that though sentences are mentioned, reality is still the whole point." This declaration by Quine could lead to calling the process of "disquotation" *semantic descent*. To talk about language is to talk about the world. This is the use of the truth predicate in Quine: "The truth predicate serves the crucial purpose, in oblique generalization, of disquotation."[9] This is especially clear in the case of logic, the site of "semantic ascent" par excellence, and for Quine the science whose statements speak less about language than about the world (11–12). Such is the radical culmination of Quine's critique of analyticity. "Logical theory, despite its heavy dependence on talk of language, is already world-oriented rather than language-oriented; and the truth predicate makes it so" (97). This particularly revealing affirmation from *Philosophy of Logic* will allow us to see the philosophical importance and radicalness of Quine's concept of truth and perhaps also what is missing from his "robust" or immanent realism.

Quine sometimes seems to be thinking of an inverted formulation of Tarski's criterion: to say that a statement is true is like saying the statement; but inversely, to say something, to say a statement, is also to say that the statement is true. To affirm a statement is at the same time to affirm the truth of the statement: we thus have the ultimate trivialization of the idea of truth and, with the idea of immanent truth, the disappearance of the question of realism. A problem remains: accounting not just for the notion of truth, but also for the predicate "true"; or, more precisely, our shared, learned usage of "true." It is not certain—and this is even an essential argument against the redundancy theory of truth à la Ramsey— that disquotation can account for this usage of "true," and it seems, to the contrary—(as Austin observed in "Truth") that in many of its current uses, the sentence "S is true" cannot be replaced by S.[10] Of course, Quine hardly liked to have recourse to ordinary language use, and I am not trying to saddle him with a type of argumentation that would be completely foreign to him. Quine always repeats that the answer to the question of truth is in science. This is exactly what he means by "truth is immanent and there is nothing above it." But then what do we mean when we say, "S is true" about a statement S? To say that truth (in general) is immanent does not tell us that truth immanent to statement S. The thesis of immanent truth, in other words, does not resolve the question of the truth of individual statements. This is another version of the holism according to which, as Quine said in "Two Dogmas," the unit of empirical meaning is science as a whole, but one cannot determine the empirical meaning of an individual statement. In the same way, one can speak of immanent truth in general, but not for a specific statement.

There would thus be two contradictory uses of the idea of immanence in Quine: "immanent truth" is a product of the naturalist use, of the integration of philosophy into science. There is no reason to go looking for truth in some first philosophy. This is a very "general" use of the terms *truth* and *immanence*. The other use, associated with Quine's utilization of Tarski, defines the truth of each statement, which is, says Quine, rendered trivial by the process of disquotation. The difficulty, I believe, is making these two trivializations of truth—one of which is carried out through naturalization (and is thus dependent on the idea of a conceptual scheme) and the other through disquotation (and is thus dependent on Quine's analysis of Tarski)—go together. They are in fact quite different.

If we follow the path of disquotation, there is indeed a trivialization of truth: to say that S is true is the same as saying S. "So far so good," says Austin. But what do we mean by that? If one speaks of the usages and circumstances of the statements S and "S is true" or "It is true that S," a series of objections present themselves, which Quine too could have formulated—for this is a problem of synonymy quite similar to the problem of the indeterminacy of translation. If one speaks of a logical procedure that passes from "S is true" to S without asking the question of meaning and usage, one can no longer count on the realist goal of the truth predicate. This is, as Quine nicely puts it, the "disappearance theory of truth."[11] Contrary to what Davidson says in "The Very Idea of a Conceptual Scheme," this version of truth undoubtedly poses more problems than the version of truth as immanent and "relative to the scheme." Indeed, the "disappearance theory of truth" empties the question of truth in the ordinary sense and in a way privileges the philosophical sense of truth. We know more or less how truth (the Truth) in general has fared since Quine (it is immanent, given by science, and so forth)—but we don't know much about the true in particular. Quine's trivialization of the idea of truth quite simply does not account for the trivial usage of "true."

All of this shows us that the question of realism is far from being resolved by Quine's definition of truth and that it is rendered even more problematic by attempts at trivializing realism via Tarski's paradigm.

Perhaps this is because to trivialize a notion is not necessarily to eliminate it. Austin himself recognizes in "Truth" that the theory of truth is a series of truisms. But these are truisms that merit exploration, and it does indeed seem that when we say "S is true" or "It is true that S" we mean something. In short, as much as the notion of truth (and of reality) is confused and almost inevitably leads—as the history of post-Quineism has shown us—to dogmatism or relativism or both, our usage of "true" seems quite well delimited and, to use one of Austin's expressions, "our size"; accessible as a given.

Perhaps it is here that we should begin: as Austin said, "*in vino*, possibly, '*veritas*,' but in a sober symposium '*verum*.' "[12] This does not mean having to give up all exploration of truth (Austin does indeed hope to clarify the question of truth), but it does mean that perhaps the best way to follow Quine's principle of immanence is to not limit oneself to his solution to the problem of truth. It is fine to say that the statement S is all we have for knowing "what we say" when we say "S is true"; indeed we have only language at our disposal to answer this question. In this respect, Austin's procedure is just as immanent as Quine's. We are within language, and there is nothing beyond it. Austin refuses, however, to stop at the Tarskian solution, while at the same time recognizing its "minimal" validity. To say that statement S is true is to state S; yes, but why stop there? Do we really know what it is to say S? Here lies the difference, to which I will return more fully, between the procedure that attends to ordinary language and an analytic method like Quine's: once the predicate "true" has been eliminated, the sentence itself remains, along with its usages, and one must indeed examine their adequacy. But above all, we can ask why it is necessary to get rid of the ordinary notion of true (the redundancy theory) or to trivialize it (Tarski's theory as taken up by Quine), when it seems in spite of everything to define something about the relation we establish between language and the world, and about the affirmation, inherent in our use of language, that language does indeed speak about something. This is just what Quine claims when he speaks of "taking our words as they are," or Davidson, when he proposes reestablishing contact with the objects that "make our statements true or false"—in short, when one or the other claims to be a realist in spite of everything. So then, why all the discussions of realism and its different species (immanent, quasi, internal), which can always be inverted into idealism or relativism? Why not stick to truth, and instead of wanting to trivialize it, try to see why it *is* trivial? After all, if there is a relationship between words and the world—and both Quine and

Davidson end up agreeing that there is, even if they sometimes do so under the threat of relativism—surely this can be called truth. The recent history of American philosophy is the history of the difficulties that arise as soon as it becomes necessary to establish, define, or rationalize this relation, and it is clear that the successive "trivializations" by Quine, Davidson, and (at the limit) Rorty have aimed at eliminating the idea of a "relation" and replacing it with "contact without mediation"; it is equally clear that they have not succeeded. Quite to the contrary, they have instead obscured our relationship to the real. At exactly the moment—between 1940 and 1950—when Quine was producing the texts that would be seminal for this entire history, Austin was proposing another path, which Quine, of course, later criticized:[13] to examine our ordinary usage of "true" and "real" in order to learn something about the relation of our language to the world. This perhaps will make it possible to answer the question of truth: indeed, says Austin, "if it is admitted (*if*) that the rather boring yet satisfactory relation between words and world which has here been discussed does genuinely occur, why should the phrase 'is true' not be our way of describing it? And if it is not, what else is?"[14]

Of course this is still trivial, but perhaps more satisfying. With this example of "truth," one begins to get a better sense of the nature of Austin's procedure: to return to ordinary language not in order to take it literally (even if it is always necessary to begin there: "The foot of the letter is the foot of the ladder")[15] but in order to see more clearly what we do in saying, for example, "S is true" or rather, "It is true that S" (since this is the more ordinary expression). Now, it quickly becomes apparent that we say "S is true" in particular circumstances where we would not be content to say S (127–28). The point appears more clearly with regard to negation. To say "S is false" is not to say the negation of S. If we follow the "redundancy theory" (let us leave the case of Tarski aside for now): "It is the same thing to say 'He is not at home' as to say 'It is false that he is at home.' (But what if no one has said that he *is* at home? What if he is lying upstairs dead?)" (127).

We can then ask whether disquotational theories, no matter what kind, are not the results of a new mythology of affirmation, from which they would derive an immanent version of truth (possibly accompanied by a myth of negation), and whether, therefore, we have not lost what we gained by eliminating the idea of representation and correspondence. Let us note that Austin, inventor of the theory of speech acts and performatives (which I will examine later) does not at all opt for a performative interpretation of "true." The status of truth in relation to performative statements is complex in another way.[16] Austin criticized Peter Strawson for precisely this interpretation in performative terms: "S is true" cannot indicate a dimension of acceptance or admission of S. The performative "I accept S," for example, does not express all we mean by "S is true." This passage from "Truth," as well as his whole polemic with Strawson,[17] demonstrates a particularity of Austin's theory for which he has been sufficiently reproached, probably as the result of a misunderstanding. Austin, while radically criticizing representationalist theories, at the same time considers it an illusion to want to abandon the idea of correspondence entirely. It is not that he wants to go back to it,[18] but he believes there is something "natural" in this idea: something essential to the functioning of our common language, something that is also found in the scientific usage of language and is probably even indispensable to it, as Quine suggested.

This has led certain of Austin's critics to attribute to him a "revised" version of correspondence. In my opinion, this is an error. Austin rejects both the notion of facts—or rather the idea that there is one fact per true statement: "for every head, the hat that goes with it"—and the notion of a "mirror" correspondence between statements and facts. Austin criticizes less the idea of an intermediary or mediation between words and the world than the idea of a "structural" or formal commonality, leveling sarcasm at Wittgenstein's *Tractatus* and its theory of representation. Signs are arbitrary, says Austin, and there is no reason why they would have anything whatsoever in common with the world, even a structure or form. For Austin, to believe as much is simply a version of Cratylism; it is to imagine that "a word needs to be echoic and writing pictographic" (here again we find the myth of meaning, which Austin also denounced, before Quine) and it is "to fall once again into the error of reading back into the world the features of language."[19] But disquotational theories of truth, which identify facts with statements and could well be the ultimate avatar of representationalism in spite of their trivial appearance, are also affected by this criticism. It seems as if we are thus faced with a grim alternative: either we say, "There is nothing there but the true statement itself, nothing to which it corresponds, or else we populate the world with linguistic *Doppelgänger* (and grossly overpopulate it ...)" (123). Austin's intuition is that these two solutions are equally erroneous. They both rest on the idea that the world resembles language because we cannot speak about the world except by using language. For Austin, contemporary conceptions of truth are based on the illusory idea that in order for there to be a relation of truth, it is necessary for there to be "something in common" between the statement and the fact—the extreme case of this parallel being disquotation, which identifies them. Austin demythologizes all this. To say that S is true is perhaps to say S, but it nevertheless remains the case that "between stating, however truly, that I am feeling sick and feeling sick there is a great gulf fixed"; or, "it takes two to make a truth" (124). One sometimes has the impression that contemporary conceptions of truth have lost sight of this point, through excessive sophistication, no doubt, and that given the choice between multiplying intermediaries (fact, meaning, intention) and the disappearance of one of the two terms (the world, for example), they have gone from "two" to (at least) three or to one.

But at this point in my analysis Austin's position is still only critical, and even if it makes it possible to see the question of realism more clearly, it does not seem to result in a convincing conception of truth or in a new version of realism. Let us now see what positive contribution this position can make, and how the philosophy of ordinary language, far from being an impasse or a *dépassé* form of the philosophy of language, can, to the contrary, put our understandings of the real and of truth back into place.

CHAPTER FOUR

Language, Facts, and Experience

In my understanding, Austin's criticisms can be conceived as a radicalization of Quine's arguments on truth and meaning; however, they call into question the thesis of immanent truth—or rather, the argument that immanent truth is a convincing answer to the question of truth. In his recent texts, Putnam has insisted on the curious convergence of "robust" realism and relativism once truth is conceived in terms of "disquotation." He is skeptical about the frequent and—for openly antirelativist philosophers like Quine, Davidson, Searle, and McDowell—even obligatory proclamation of the will to reestablish "unmediated contact" between language and the world; in short, the proclamation of "direct realism." Tarski's theory—which of course I cannot comment on in depth here—thus serves handily for calling oneself a realist, whereas, precisely, *saying it is not enough* (that would be too easy). "There is less to some versions of 'direct realism' than meets the eye. Sometimes the term is applied to any position that denies that the objects of 'veridical' perception are sense data. Such a usage makes it much too easy to be a direct realist. All one has to do to be a direct realist (in *this* sense) about visual experience, for example, is to say, 'We don't *perceive* visual experiences, we *have* them.' A simple linguistic reform, and *voila!* one is a direct realist."[1]

This type of linguistic reform seems to be perfectly illustrated by the now-classical recourse to Tarski for a "deflationist" definition of truth and a ready-made realism. As Putnam remarks a bit further on, it would be curious if progress were so easily achieved in philosophy. The question of perception is not settled by the simple affirmation that we see objects directly,[2] nor is the question of truth made moot by the affirmation that we speak directly about the world without mediation. We still have to know—and this is precisely the point that aroused Austin's formidable irony in *Sense and Sensibilia*—what is meant by "directly." First of all, this "directly" is clearly of the order, once again, of "wishful thinking," as long as the argument of direct realism is accompanied by an entire theoretical arsenal including regimentation and canonical notation, the theory of reference, the production of beliefs, and the optimization of agreement, to choose just a few concepts at random. Having eliminated a certain number of intermediary entities does not guarantee us directness. Next, "directly" is meaningful only in relation to "indirectly," and thus its usage in the absolute is problematic, according to Austin. What is it, or what would it be, anyway, to see "indirectly" or to speak indirectly about the world?

One of the incontestable advantages of Quine's thesis of indeterminacy—which constitutes its radicalness—is, as we have seen, that it constitutes a magnificent critique of meaning, along with its corollary, a critique of the notion of fact. One of Quine's most brilliant passages is thus the opening of *Philosophy of Logic*. I detect in it something of Austin's tone in "Truth"—an essay that Quine commented on at an American Philosophical Association symposium dedicated to Austin's methods in 1965,[3] several years before Quine delivered his lectures on logic. (In his talk Quine mentions Austin's "scintillating" essay on truth—of course before criticizing it.)

When someone speaks truly, what makes his statement true? We tend to feel that there are two factors: meaning and fact. A German utters a declarative sentence: "*Der Schnee ist Weiss*." In so doing he speaks truly, thanks to the happy concurrence of two circumstances: his sentence means that snow is white, and in point of fact snow *is* white. If meanings had been different, if "*weiss*" had meant green, then in uttering what he did he would not have spoken truly. If the facts had been different, if snow had been red, then again he would not have spoken truly.

What I have just said has a reassuring air of platitude about it, and at the same time it shows disturbing signs of philosophical extravagance. The German utters his declarative sentence; also there is this white snow all around; so far so good.[4] But must we go on and appeal also to intangible intervening elements, a meaning and a fact? The *meaning* of the *sentence* is that snow is white, and the *fact* of the *matter* is that snow is white. The meaning of the sentence and the fact of the matter here are apparently identical, or at any rate they have the same name: that snow is white.

. . . This has the ring of a correspondence theory of truth, but as a theory it is a hollow mockery. The correspondence holds only between two intangibles that we have invoked as intervening elements between the German sentence and the white snow.[5]

Here, we find the antimetaphysical radicalness of Austin's essay and a double criticism: of meaning and of fact. But just as Quine does not have a problem with signification or meaning in the ordinary sense, as we have seen, but only takes aim at philosophers' significations (notably, the Fregean idea of *Sinn*), so he does not have a problem with, for example, the ordinary usage of "the fact that," but rather with the philosophical conception of facts. Facts, like meanings, do not exist independently of statements, and Quine prefers not to have recourse to a universe of separate facts. Here his arguments join with Austin's mentioned above. But Quine has a problem in general with any hypostasis of facts on the basis of statements. From that perspective, one must also reject certain criticisms of facts that seek to eliminate them on the basis of the notion of thoughts or, obviously, propositions. Frege, already a target of the critique of the myth of meaning, remarked with irony, " 'Facts, facts, facts' cries the scientist when he wants to emphasize the necessity of a firm foundation for science. What is a fact? A fact is a thought that is true."[6] It seems that hardly any light is shed on the notion of fact by saying this, and that, as Austin would say, this definition no longer has anything to do with our ordinary usage of "fact." But above all, defining facts as immanent to our statements risks being just as problematic as positing them as intermediary "phantoms" between statements and reality.

One may also think of the proposition-thought in the *Tractatus* in relation to Quine's critique of facts (even if Wittgenstein does not count on this notion in order to define facts or states of affairs, which in the *Tractatus* are primary). Quine criticizes the idea that it is possible to assign a determined state of affairs to a statement. He seems to repeat Austin's argument (for every hat, the head it belongs to), but in reality his target is something else. Quine began criticizing the notion of fact as early as 1934, the publication date of one of his first articles, "Ontological Remarks on the Propositional Calculus,"[7] and already there his arguments make it clear that the problem for him is not so much facts as *propositions*—that is, Bertrand Russell. Thus, in the first lines of *Philosophy of Logic*, which I quoted earlier, Quine presents himself as "inveighing against propositions."[8] For Quine, the proposition combines the flaws of both the notion of meaning and the notion of fact. Moreover, in 1941 Quine published a criticism of Russell's *An Inquiry into Meaning and Truth* in which he noted the mysteriousness of the correspondence between truth and fact in Russell.[9] He persisted with this criticism and concluded it in 1966, in an article later included in *Theories and Things*, "Russell's Ontological Development," in which he mercilessly traces the history of Russell's gradual attraction to an ontology of facts.[10]

As always with Quine (as we have already observed with regard to truth), things become quite different when envisioned no longer in relation to statements but within the framework of holism and conceptual schemes. Indeed, Quine pursues his critique of facts at the epistemological level, and his fundamental text "Two Dogmas of Empiricism" can be read as much as a critique of factuality as of analyticity. We find once again in Quine the desire to criticize meaning and fact in parallel, but the two entities appear here as (indeterminable) components of statements. It was Carnap—as Quine himself noted—who best understood the foundation of the Quinean position: he writes in a note in *Empiricism, Semantics and Ontology*, "Quine does not acknowledge the distinction which I emphasize above, because according to him there are no sharp boundary lines between logical and factual truth, between questions of meaning and questions of fact."[11] As Carnap's remark makes clear, this is Quine's *general* position. "The truth of statements does obviously depend both on language and upon extralinguistic fact."[12] Quine returns to this double dependence, which is at the center of his philosophy, in his essay "Carnap and Logical Truth." But again, the problem is to see the meaning of this duality—quite comprehensible within the framework of science in general—for a particular statement.

The epistemological sense of this double dependence is clear. It is precisely what Quine's holism, and what is referred to as the Duhem-Quine thesis, amount to. Quine does not take up the details of Duhem's arguments so much as the general "philosophy" of *La théorie physique* (*The Aim and Structure of Physical Theory*), in particular the impossibility of conceiving facts independently of all conceptualization. This is a central point in Duhem's book, the first work to present and argue this thesis fully. "What the physicist states as the result of an experiment," writes Duhem in a famous passage, "is not the recital of observed facts, but the interpretation and transposing of these facts into the ideal, abstract, symbolic world created by the theories he regards as established."[13] Quine takes up this point as is—for him, a statement of experience independent of all theoretical context is an epistemological myth. With the exception of a few collectors' items for epistemologists, statements are connected to experience only in a roundabout way. Thus the idea, shared by Quine, Kuhn, and Paul Feyerabend and later criticized by Davidson and McDowell, that the "given" is immediately theorized comes from Duhem. For Duhem himself, this theorization takes place under the notion of *translation*.

Indeed, from Duhem—who was on this point the inspiration for American epistemologists—onward, we notice the development of the double sense of translation, linguistic and epistemological, present in Quine *and* Kuhn. This proximity between Quine and Kuhn regarding questions of *translation*, and not simply conceptual schemes, appears very clearly in Kuhn's text "Reflections on my Critics."[14] In fact, Kuhn takes up this theme of translation and demonstrates the kinship between his own arguments and Quine's. He also responds to an objection by Popper, who, before Davidson, criticized the "Myth of the Framework,"[15] that is, the myth of the frame of reference, which Kuhn defines as the "the dogma that the different frameworks are like mutually untranslatable languages," whereas "the fact is that even totally different languages (like English and Hopi, or Chinese) are not untranslatable."[16] According to Kuhn, Quine did in fact state precisely the problem of the incommensurability of paradigms, even if he would not express it in those terms. To write the history of a science is to translate its discourses into *our* terms. We translate "older theories into modern terms" (269) and thus we learn, for example, how to read documents differently. "Learning to translate a language or a theory is learning to describe the world with which the language or theory functions." To know a paradigm is thus to measure its distance from us and to "acquire the knowledge of nature that is built into language" (270). This learning is like learning a foreign language, and, as with radical translation, one can learn, "with time and skill," to predict the reactions of the other, to know not his world but the relation between his world and our own, "something that the historian regularly learns to do (or should) when dealing with older scientific theories" (277). From this perspective, which Ian Hacking takes up in his essay "Five Parables,"[17] we have access to a distant world (either in space or in time) through a process of translation, because our knowledge itself is a translation from a given into a theory. The two processes of translation are subject to indeterminacy—certainly differently in Duhem than in his Anglo-Saxon successors.

This idea of the theorization of the given is obviously at the origin of a number of difficulties raised by the question of realism, and, combined with the thesis of indeterminacy that I have already examined, it calls into question the very starting point of Quine's philosophy: the notion of experience, and more specifically the notion of an "observation sentence."

Our experience is conceptualized from the beginning: "Conceptualization on any considerable scale is inseparable from language."[18] A statement like "the current is on"[19] or "green stain now"—"the very type of event that fills the epistemologist's heart with joy"—is for Quine theoretical, just as all our objects, including the ordinary ones, are theoretical. "Obviously the truth of the most casually factual sentence depends partly on language."[20] This defines what we may call Quine's "gradualism," which runs throughout his epistemology following "The Two Dogmas of Empiricism" and which I will not discuss here, as the arguments are well known.

The more specific, "ontological" sense of Quine's critique of facts is, in my opinion, more difficult to apprehend and put into relation with the more general duality of the factual and the theoretical—so much so that one may wonder to what extent the problem is the same. It is clear that the idea of a theorized given and the impossibility of "brute" facts is at the base of a certain form of idealism, or, to use Hacking's expression, nominalism. Now, in the case of Kuhn, for example, we find a very general, holistic argument that does not seem to bear on the particular statements of a science but on the overall historicity of our relationship to nature and the problems this raises for reading scientific texts from the past. The idea of incommensurability has thus given rise to misunderstandings, because it has several uses: first, historical incommensurability, which affirms that in changing theories one "changes subject" and explains the world with new concepts that are incompatible with the preceding ones. This incommensurability, already remarkably thematized by Meyerson and Duhem, is not an obstacle but, as Kuhn himself acknowledges, a task and a concern for the history of science.[21] Another use of incommensurability is more clearly linked to the indeterminacy of reference in Quine, and it radicalizes the historical one. This is undoubtedly the use of incommensurability Davidson targets in his criticism of conceptual schemes. It no longer bears on theories, but on the entities theories speak of. As Putnam shows, the reference of the word *water*, for example (once there are successive and radically incommensurable scientific conceptions of it), is an especially difficult matter, on which it is perhaps impossible to come to any conclusion whatsoever. This difficulty leads to two positions: internal realism (which is no longer anything but ersatz realism) and, in Quine, frank indifference: the absence of a "fact of the matter" of the question. This attitude brings the question of reference and scientific realism close to the thesis of the indeterminacy of translation. The possibility of having several competing theories of the world, all of which explain experience, disappears on account of their equivalence, on account of indeterminacy itself.[22] We move from the problem of the truth of theories to the problem of the existence of theoretical entities. This leads Hacking, for example, to distinguish between two sorts of realism,[23] one of which bears on theories and the other on entities.

It is exactly in this shift from one problem to another (very different) problem that the source of the difficulties seems to reside. It is a central, even initial, point of empiricism that there are several possible manners of explaining the given. The simple observation of science's practices shows (as Duhem said) that the given is theorized. Is it necessary, for all that, to deduce that since the objects of science are radically indeterminate (because even the idea of *what can count as an object* evolves), there is a fundamental problem in our ordinary relation to objects and in our relation to ordinary objects? The continuity that, based on Quine, I have maintained between these two categories of objects, scientific and ordinary, would seem to push us in this direction. But in fact, there is no reason that this continuity would always go in the same direction and transfer the difficulties of the language of science—or rather, not exactly the language of science but a certain formalization of it—into ordinary language. Hacking criticizes those uses (shared by Quine and Putnam) of the Löwenheim-Skolem thesis that lead to maintaining that any domain of objects can be assigned to a theory and that the difference between two ontological choices will never appear (see Quine's theory of "proxy functions" in *Theories and Things* and Putnam's "Models and Reality")[24]—which is a simple and radical way of expressing the indeterminacy of reference. Now, the majority of arguments against naive (let us say, correspondence) realism are in this way inseparable from a prior theorization (regimentation or formalization) of language. One question then becomes inevitable. Aren't arguments against realism (or for realism "nevertheless"—they are often the same thing) the "immanent" product of the formalization of language? It is not a matter here (it would be too simple) of contrasting ordinary language and some realism proper to it to the antirealism that would emerge once one examines the language of science and its "position" on objects: again, there is nothing that says our ordinary language is more realist than the language of science (that would be, once more, a *petitio principii*), or that our language functions within a realist "background," to use Searle's terminology.[25] It is instead a matter of reexamining the nature of facts and truth—not the truth of theories in general, but of particular statements: perhaps it is possible to learn something from them about the objects of which they speak. No principle of antiformalism guides my approach here (nor the approach of ordinary language philosophers, not for the most part, at any rate), but rather a bewilderment concerning problematics that turn out to depend entirely on a certain way of conceiving and constituting language—which would be of little importance if these problematics did not lead to impasses.

As I have suggested several times, what is radical in Quine is the critique of the myth of meaning that the thesis of the indeterminacy of translation performs; it is this critique that, for the majority of Quine's interpreters, calls realism into question. However, it is clear—see the passage from *Philosophy of Logic* cited earlier—that Quine's critique bears more on the notion of meaning than on the notion of fact, which he quickly stopped discussing. It is true that a strict parallel between meaning and fact cannot be established, and there is an important difference in perspective between the beginning of *Philosophy of Logic* and "Two Dogmas." One might think that the rejection of the analytic-synthetic distinction is a double criticism of both the notions of meaning and of fact, and this is a seductive idea, since in decreeing that the two dogmas are "at root identical," Quine rejects at the same time the idea of an isolatable linguistic *and* factual component of statements. However, this is not the case, and meaning is much more frequently called into question in Quine than is the notion of fact, which is all the more remarkable considering that Quine also uses the notion of "fact of the matter" (which has been much discussed, and I will not focus on it here).[26] It seems, then, that it is possible to separate the two problems. Quine is obviously opposed to any creation of a "world" or ontology of facts parallel to the world of meanings, whose function (like that of meanings) would be to artificially procure an "assurance of determinacy" between the statements of different languages.[27] But he has nothing against the ordinary notion of fact, just as in the "myth of meaning" his target was not the ordinary sense of *mean*. His obstinate preservation of the notion of observation sentences—which continues through his most recent texts, in spite of his strengthening of the arguments of indeterminacy—seems to go in this direction.

Whatever Quine's position may in fact be—and it seems that here his position is not so determined—one may ask, at the risk of appearing to be fighting a losing battle, whether the notion of fact can be so easily eliminated from philosophy. It is clear that this notion was seriously called into question from the moment ideas of correspondence and of the analytic-synthetic distinction began to be questioned in various ways. But it is possible to try to save facts without thereby returning to an ontology of facts or to a myth of correspondence (for every hat, its head) or to the myth of statements of nontheorized experience (the myth of the given), simply by basing oneself on a certain use of language: the fact is that we talk about facts (and not only about *objects*, despite what Quine and Strawson, after him, say). It is not because we know how to ask and explain what a word or sentence means that we are doomed to recognize or invent the world of meanings; in the same way, it is not because we speak of facts and refer to facts that we have recourse to an ontology of facts. What characterizes the ordinary notion of facts is precisely that they are not *always* well determined or described by language; this is even almost never the case, which is exactly what Austin means when he condemns Strawson's attitude as being "Unfair to Facts."[28]

Let us return to what I said a bit earlier about Austin's "rehabilitation" of a certain form of correspondence. As we have seen, Austin criticizes above all the idea (sometimes inherent to the concept of correspondence) of the existence of one and only one fact corresponding to every true statement. What is false in the idea of correspondence is the ontological assumption of a world of facts, and especially the thesis of a "mirror" relation according to which statements reproduce the traits (the structure or form) of reality. What is true in the idea of correspondence is the idea of a correlation between statements and words and a situation. For Austin, there is a correlation between true sentences and "the *types* of situation, thing, event, etc. to be found in the world."[29] This correlation is based, among other things, on what he calls "descriptive conventions." For the moment, let us say that for Austin this correlation is both more arbitrary ("We are absolutely free to appoint *any* symbol to describe *any* type of situation" [124]) and more serious than philosophers usually believe: "There must be something other than the words, which the words are to be used to communicate about: this may be called the 'world'" (121).

Austin considers that philosophers of logic are uselessly formalist when they exclude facts from "what is part of the world" and keep only things, objects, and so forth. Indeed, Quine insisted on the objectival scheme, and we know that the entire process of "regimentation" in quantification is based on the first thesis of "On What There Is": what exists is everything. Very well: nevertheless, we do also speak of facts, and one cannot easily make them disappear (even if Austin does not say that we posit the *existence* of facts). It is not enough to say that a fact is simply a "true statement" to get out of this situation—it doesn't take Austin many examples to show that this is not the case.

Here again the disagreement takes on an ontological aspect, as the rest of the debate seems to confirm. Inverting a proposition from the *Trac-*

tatus, Strawson affirms clearly that "the world is the totality of things, not of facts"[30] and refuses to include facts among the "things that are in the world." Davidson later takes up this theme, notably in "True to the Facts," the title of which refers back to Austin's title, "Unfair to Facts." It is astonishing that this kinship between Austin and Davidson (which can be explained historically) is almost never pointed out by commentators, whereas it is clear that, just as in the essay "The Very Idea of a Conceptual Scheme," here too Davidson's critical radicalness comes directly out of Austin's arguments in "Truth." It is true that Davidson's reinterpretation of Austin's conceptions—within the framework of his new theory of meaning, which originated from Tarski's "convention T"—loses the essential part of its initial radicalness and, as we have seen, arrives at a realism of pure form ("minimal," as it is often called) with which I do not want to be satisfied any more than Austin does.

The defense of facts produced by Austin has been widely attacked, to such an extent that it has been practically forgotten today,[31] inasmuch as the scheme of objectival quantification and Quine's criticism of the ontology of facts, having rejected the ontology of the *Tractatus*, seem to have gotten the better of facts. However, I believe—following Cora Diamond or James Conant[32]—that there is something very important in the *Tractatus*'s approach, which is not refuted by the method later adopted by Wittgenstein and which has to do with realism (or rather, as Diamond would say, with the "realistic spirit," for it is not certain that realism as a *thesis* can be defended in Wittgenstein or in Austin—despite what Searle suggests). And there is certainly proximity between Austin's defense of facts, situations, states of affairs, and so forth, and Wittgenstein's position in the *Tractatus*. What is false in the *Tractatus*'s idea of states of affairs, and was subsequently abandoned by Wittgenstein, is its implication of a structural similarity and a necessary correlation between a proposition and a situation. For Austin, as for Wittgenstein in the *Blue Book* and in the *Investigations*, understanding the nature of language means seeing that this correlation can always be made in various ways and is never perfect—which for Wittgenstein amounts to abandoning the "*preconceived idea* of crystalline purity" of logic,[33] and for Austin means realizing that even a language "developed" and logicized so as to "'mirror' in conventional ways features described in the world" does not make it possible to solve the problem of the truth of statements, which remains a matter of "the words used being the ones *conventionally appointed* for situations of the type to which that referred to belongs."[34] Thus, what is true in the

Tractatus's theory, and remains constant in Wittgenstein's later method, is the idea of a relation of adequacy between statements and the world (facts) that is *nowhere else* than in language[35]—an entirely nonmetaphysical theory of truth. Of course, theories of immanent truth or reinterpretations of truth à la Tarski also pursue this antimetaphysical aim (for the most part). But they lose something that Austin constantly points out: the ordinary obviousness of a *difference* between the saying and the fact—and thus, they lose the problem itself: "between stating, however truly,[36] that I am feeling sick and feeling sick there is a great gulf fixed."[37] This is a truism, but one that is sometimes forgotten in theorizations of truth and is above all perfectly *shown* in our ordinary notion of *fact*.

> "Fact that" is a phrase designed for use in situations where the distinction between a true statement and the state of affairs about which it is a truth is neglected; as it often is with advantage in ordinary life, though seldom in philosophy.
>
> ... To ask "Is the fact that S the true statement that S or that which it is true of?" may beget absurd answers. To take an analogy: although we may sensibly ask "Do we *ride* the word 'elephant' or the animal?" and equally sensibly "Do we *write* the word or the animal?" it is nonsense to ask "Do we *define* the word or the animal?" For defining an elephant (supposing we ever do this) is a compendious description of an operation involving both word and animal (do we focus on the image or the battleship?); and so speaking about "the fact that" is a compendious way of speaking about a situation involving both words and world.[38]

In his usual casual tone, Austin proposes a remarkable solution to the question of "realism," all the while showing that most philosophical formulations of the question are hardly reasonable and are even nonsense, since they consist in asking whether (or affirming that) in speaking about a statement S, one is speaking about what S says. The ordinary notion of fact (what we mean when we say "the fact that," "it is a fact," "let us look at the facts," etc.) indeed shows that these formulations create a false problem—which does not mean that truth itself is a *Scheinproblem*, but rather that it is not explained either by "disquotation" or in general by a semantic theory that would seek to eliminate the expressions "is true" or "is a fact." Austin does not proclaim an ontology of facts (what would that mean for him?) but maintains that it is curious to exclude facts from "things-in-the-world," even if there is an important (logical) difference between, for example, facts, events, and phenomena. "It seems to me, on the contrary, that to say that something is a fact *is* at least in part precisely to say that it is something in the world,"[39] says Austin, who remarks on this occasion that our uses of the expression "to be a fact" resemble our uses of "to exist" (in that, as we know, existence is not a predicate). With this type of remark, Austin seems to stop short of existential quantification, which would disqualify him in the eyes of many from discussing truth.[40] But, I believe, the situation is quite the opposite—and for me this is what is interesting in Austin's analysis: these remarks indeed indicate where and how to look for something like realism. It is just as bizarre, Austin remarks, to say "facts are things-in-the-world" as it is to say "entities are things-in-the-world," because to say that something is a fact (like saying: "this is a person") is "at least in part precisely to say that it is something in the world" (it is an oxymoron to speak of an imaginary fact or person). Whence Austin's "speculation" "that it could be shown that some of the odd phenomena notorious about the word 'fact' could be shown to be connected with this 'existential' side of it (some of which, however, have been much exaggerated!)."[41] We *talk about facts* and not, for Austin, only about such or such "fact that." And statements can "correspond" to or rather (because correspondence is problematic) can be more or less adequate to the facts ("fitting the facts," an expression Austin considers not sufficiently examined, especially in Strawson).

Thus, Austin retains something of correspondence truth (Strawson attributes to him a "purified version of the correspondence theory of truth,"[42] and this is the project later taken up by Davidson),[43] but he shows that by examining our ordinary usages of "true" and "fact," it is possible to give this theory a reasonable meaning. This gives our ordinary notions of fact and of true (or, as in *Sense and Sensibilia*, of "real") something we would be tempted to call a realist scope, if Austin himself had not mocked the expression. Those in the United States today who have the great (and all too rare) merit of going back to Austin in order to rethink and refound realism—Putnam and, in a still more developed way, Searle—either in terms of "natural realism" or "background" perhaps miss the very radicalness of Austin's argumentation and the meaning of his return to ordinary language. Our *usages* are not more realist than antirealist, and it does indeed seem today that by formulating the problem of the relation of *words* to *world* in this way (that is, in the form of an alternative between realism and antirealism, which has become more complex over the course of the years), analytic discussions have exhausted themselves.

CHAPTER FIVE

Empiricism Again

W hat sense is there in posing the *question* of realism? For Austin, probably none whatsoever, and even less in advocating a "modest" or "naive" realism (both of these qualifications, when used in philosophy, mean exactly the opposite of what they ordinarily mean), or even a "direct" realism (the expression used by Putnam and Bouveresse). What, asks Austin, would indirect realism be? And in general, can we say that we see (or more broadly, perceive) directly or indirectly? To return to the passage cited earlier, "do we focus on the image or the battleship?"[1] This brings us back to the question of empiricism, with which we are clearly not yet finished.

A superficial reading of *Sense and Sensibilia*, Austin's least understood work, might lead one to believe that Austin defends a linguistic or language-based theory of perception. But it is quite the opposite. Austin rejects the idea (which is so widespread that to call it into question seems either incongruous or reactionary) that our perception is *dependent* on language. But he does not say, *for all that*, that perception is *independent* of language—to the contrary, these two opposing arguments share the same defect (a fundamental point for Austin): first, they are typically philosophical arguments that not only neglect the ordinary use of language but even pervert it ("abuse it," to take an important concept from *How to Do Things with Words*; here, when one abuses ordinary language, one *pays* for it);[2] and next, they rest on the same metaphysical presupposition: that the relation between language and perception can be examined, evaluated, or discussed. This is why it would be false to say that Austin defends a form of naive realism; first, because there is nothing *naive* about his realism; next, because according to him there is hardly any sense in speaking of realism; and finally, because Austin does not think there is anything to *defend* here, since for him it is language that must be defended against philosophy and theses like realism and antirealism. In *Sense and Sensibilia* Austin explicitly attacks the doctrine that "we never see or otherwise perceive (or 'sense'), or anyhow we never *directly* perceive or sense, material objects (or material things) but only sense-data" (2), and so forth.

It is not my goal here to elaborate Austin's criticism of this doctrine, nor more generally to treat the problem of perception, which is far too vast and which I have not explored in detail in my work.[3] I would simply like to use Austin once more to demonstrate the inanity, or at least the difficulty, of certain problematics—not only those Austin was specifically aiming at (Ayer and Price's), but in general all doctrines that want to base antirealism or realism (in various forms) on a theory of perception. Indeed, for Austin discussions of realism are rooted in "scholastic views" and artificial dichotomies that result from philosophy's "old habits of *Gleichschaltung*"[4] (which, by the way, have developed significantly since his time).

> I am *not*, then—and this is a point to be clear about from the beginning—going to maintain that we ought to be "realists," to embrace, that is, the doctrine that we *do* perceive material things (or objects). This doctrine would be no less scholastic and erroneous than its antithesis. The question, do we perceive material things or sense-data, no doubt looks very simple—*too* simple—but is entirely misleading. . . . One of the most important points to grasp is that these two terms "sense-data" and "material things," live by taking in each other's washing—what is spurious is not one term of the pair, but the antithesis itself. (3–4)

Obviously, in the time since Ayer and Price's propositions and Austin's criticism of them, much water has passed under the bridge, and the problematic has been greatly modified and in any case perfected, if one may say so: there is no longer a distinct opposition between sense data and material things; instead, as we have seen, there is talk of notions of content, mental acts, and intentionality on the one hand, and notions of world, matter, or simply nature on the other. However, the dualism (mind–the world) has not budged, and contrary to what one sometimes reads, it is to be feared that Austin's arguments still apply.

It is sometimes said that alleged advances in the science of perception have invalidated Austin's arguments. David Marr, for example, quotes Austin and writes that his objections to theories of perceptions would today be unfounded since we are now much better able to describe the forms of objects and the processes of perceiving them (our perception of the

"real form" of a cat, to take the example from Austin that Marr criticizes).[5]
Certainly since the 1950s, when Austin was teaching the material for *Sense
and Sensibilia*, "it has appeared that a good number of the problems that
might at first glance seem insoluble and to justify a skeptical attitude like
Austin's could be resolved perfectly."[6] But in reality *this changes nothing*
for the problem Austin posed, which is more fundamental. "It is certainly
not obvious that an improved scientific understanding of processes like
perception must at the same time constitute a solution to the difficult and
profound philosophical problems that have, from the beginning, been
posed with regard to perception—problems that have a distressing tendency to reappear constantly in different forms, preferring to do so where
one least expects them, and which are certainly much more resistant than
is generally supposed; nor is it self-evident that this understanding might
even bring us any closer to the solution being sought" (207).

The criticisms in *Sense and Sensibilia*, which were aimed squarely at the
empiricist tradition, are perhaps even more useful now that the scheme
of perception has been elaborated and empiricism itself abandoned, described successively as dogmatic, mythical, or outmoded, in order to set in
opposition, quite simply, "mind" and "world." McDowell is a rather typical
example of these simplifications, which, as a result of wanting to "reduce"
the number of theoretical instruments involved, lead either to overly sophisticated conceptions or simply, as Bouveresse and later Crispin Wright
have pointed out, to a rather classical form of idealism. Many reductionist
positions (which want to eliminate "the given," "facts," and so forth) are
open to the same reproach, for they lead inevitably either to a catch-all
concept of intentionality (which recuperates both mind and world) or to a
so-called direct realism that is in fact a realism of pure form—"spurious"
according to Austin.

The argument of "progress" achieved or about to be achieved by science also plays a fundamental role in the idea, found in many present-day
conceptions, that certain difficult philosophical problems (the nature of
representation, of perception, of thought, among others) are destined to
disappear or be explained definitively. Austin's merit is to show that once
these questions are posed in a certain way, they cannot be resolved—at
least not in the terms, dichotomies, and problematics imposed by philosophy. "So we are *not* to look for an answer to the question, what kind of
thing we perceive,"[7] a question that is in any case absurd, although it has
been asked in a great many recent analytic publications. Before Austin,
Wittgenstein discussed a type of scientistic argumentation that takes for

granted that philosophical difficulties (in his case, the functioning of the mind) will be resolved "later." "Someday perhaps we shall know more about them—we think. But that is just what commits us to a particular way of looking at the matter. For we have a definite concept of what it means to learn to know a process better. (The decisive movement in the conjuring trick has been made, and it was the very one that we thought quite innocent.)"[8]

We may wonder, then, whether current discussions of perception (for example, the question of preconceptualization or "prestructuration" of the perceptual given, the question of meaning included within perception, or the question of the relation between perception and the object perceived) do not start off from a false question, as Hacker, Putnam, and Bouveresse have all suggested in different ways—a question that simply hijacks the ordinary uses of *to see*, *to perceive*, and even *real*. This reproach could be extended to many discussions of realism. In the preface to his French translation of *Sense and Sensibilia*, Paul Gochet noted that Austin constantly decries the abuse of ordinary language by philosophy—not so much because philosophy forgets ordinary language, but because it exploits it, taking liberties with language and taking the natural uses of language for its own artificial, contrived use. In this way, *Sense and Sensibilia* develops points already formulated in "Other Minds." The philosopher asks, "How can I know" or "How do I know" that there is a real goldfinch, whereas this question—"How do you know?"—can be asked (in ordinary language) only in certain contexts, and precisely those in which one is in a position to dispel doubt (about whether the bird is stuffed, for example).[9]

> The doubt or question "But is it a *real* one?" has always (*must* have) a special basis, there must be some "reason for suggesting" that it isn't real, in the sense of some specific way, or limited number of specific ways, in which it is suggested that this experience or item may be phoney. . . .
>
> If the context doesn't make it clear, then I am entitled to ask "How do you mean? Do you mean it may be stuffed or what? *What are you suggesting?*" The wile of the metaphysician consists in asking "Is it a real table?" (a kind of object which has no obvious way of being phoney) and not specifying or limiting what may be wrong with it, so that I feel at a loss "how to prove" it *is* a real one. It is the use of the word "real" in this manner that leads us on to the suspicion that "real" has a single meaning ("the real world," "material objects"), and that a highly profound and puzzling one. Instead, we should insist always on specifying with what "real" is being contrasted.[10]

This Austinian analysis of "real"[11] is taken up and developed in *Sense and Sensibilia* with particular force in chapter 7 (a chapter that inspired, among others, Hacking in *Representing and Intervening* and Putman in his Dewey Lectures). At the beginning of *Sense and Sensibilia*, Austin takes issue with the notion of "sense datum," which Moore and Russell introduced in order to avoid the problems raised by the notion of sensation, by thus specifying its "content" (an absolute premise that would, in a way, escape the relativity of sensation). The idea that we can examine our sensations (or strip them down in such a way as to be able to obtain sense data, which for Austin amounts to the same thing) is "the original sin (Berkeley's apple, the tree in the quad) by which the philosopher casts himself out from the garden of the world we live in."[12] The illusion Austin condemns is twofold: first, it is the illusion that I have a better chance of reaching "the real" by speaking about sense data than by speaking about objects and following the ordinary rules of language, and second, the illusion that there is a univocal definition of "real." For Austin the language of sense data is by no means the absolute premise dreamed of by empiricists but a secondary and derivative idiom; not a primary, "incorrigible" language but a secondary, diminished form of language. Quine later took up this point very lucidly in his response to Davidson, "On the Very Idea of a Third Dogma," although Quine himself often speaks of sensory givens or "surface irritations": "Our typical sentences are about bodies and substances, assumed or known in varying degrees, out in the world. Typically they are not about sense data or experiences or, certainly, surface irritations. . . . Nobody could suppose that I supposed that people are on the whole talking about their nerve endings.[13] That having been said, the philosophers who really try to take such a fact seriously are rare indeed; Quine at any rate thinks that once one takes on the ontological question, it is no longer a matter of ordinary language. At the least, he does not believe that philosophy must improve or clear up some ordinary or natural ontology. "Ontological concern is not a correction of a lay thought and practice; it is foreign to the lay culture, though an outgrowth of it" (9). Others have fewer scruples and were already ridiculed in *Sense and Sensibilia*. It is not Ayer's position as such that Austin criticizes, but rather a certain way of posing problems that allegedly arise "from ordinary opinion" (for example, the ordinary opinion that we "really" see things) but in fact arise from a pure construction. This is a way, says Austin, to "soften up the plain man's alleged views for the subsequent treatment; it is preparing the way for, by practically attributing to *him*, the so-called philosophers' view."[14] In short, a procedure like Ayer's, Austin's target at the beginning of chapter 2 of *Sense and Sensibilia*, unites several features:

1. A certain condescension toward the ordinary man: "Is it not rather delicately hinted in this passage that the plain man is really a bit naïve? It 'does not normally occur' to him that his belief in 'the existence of material things' needs justifying—but perhaps it *ought* to occur to him."[15] This condescension is evidently linked to the way the ordinary man's opinion is formulated:[16] "Though ostensibly the plain man's position here is just being described, a little quiet undermining is already being effected by these turns of phrase."[17] Reading these gibes by Austin, one cannot help but think that they would apply especially well (perhaps even more than to empiricist doctrines) to the way current mentalist doctrines appeal to pop or folk psychology—an appeal to a paper tiger that is regularly deflated by genuine doctrines of the mental. As Vincent Descombes has noted: "At first, the mentalist dogma is presented as something exceedingly ordinary, something like the mere recognition of the existence of a psychological dimension to human affairs. Who, other than an outmoded, narrow-minded behaviorist, would dare deny that people have opinions and desires? . . . Who is willing to reject the platitude according to which people act on their beliefs or towards what they seek to achieve? Yet, in the end the reader is surprised to learn that, by assenting to these obvious truths, he has gradually embraced the elements of a particular metaphysics of mind."[18]

2. Another flaw, which is linked to the first: if one were to ask the ordinary man whether a chair in front of him exists and whether he sees it, he "would regard doubt in such a case, not as far-fetched or over-refined or somehow unpractical, but as plain *nonsense*." Thus, "it is misleading to hint, not only that there is always room for doubt, but that the philosophers' dissent from the plain man is just a matter of degree; it is really not *that* kind of disagreement at all."[19] The error (or fraud) consists in arguing the philosopher's position against the ordinary position (possibly even strengthening it, which is the same thing), whereas if such an ordinary position exists, it is not on the same level. Wittgenstein would say that it is a matter of two different grammars.

3. Third point: the philosopher introduces certain entities *into* the ordinary man's opinion (for example, sense-perception: "We think [according to Ayer] that, in general, our 'sense-perceptions' can 'be trusted'").[20] Austin criticized, just as Quine did later, the introduction of fictive and dubious entities such as meanings into philosophy (notably in "The

Meaning of a Word").[21] But there is a further point here: these entities are arbitrarily attributed to the ordinary man in order to then reject, amend, or clarify his opinion. "These entities, which of course don't really figure at all in the plain man's language or among his beliefs, are brought in with the implication that whenever we 'perceive' there is an *intermediate* entity *always* present and *informing* us about something *else*.[22]

Here again we find a move that has not disappeared since Austin and has even gained strength with mentalist theories, which are almost always based on the attribution of *beliefs* to the ordinary psychological subject. Of course, it sometimes happens that the ordinary man considers himself to have been "deceived," but "talk of deception only *makes sense* against a background of general non-deception. (You can't fool all of the people all of the time)."[23] What is more, for the ordinary man, "to be deceived" (by a magician's trick or by his fuel gauge) does not mean for him "to perceive something non-real."[24] There are differences among errors (see the analysis of the difference between illusion and delusion).[25] This is how Austin most clearly expresses this point, which sums up, if you will, his *realism*: "Looking at the Müller-Lyer diagram (in which, of two lines of equal length, one looks longer than the other), or at a distant village on a very clear day across a valley is a very different kettle of fish from seeing a ghost or from having D.T.s and seeing pink rats. And when the plain man sees on the stage the Headless Woman, what he sees (and this *is* what he sees, whether he knows it or not) is not something 'unreal' or 'immaterial,' but a woman against a dark background with her head in a black bag" (14).

In short, seeing is seeing and nothing else (not seeing or even *having* perceptions, whether deceptive or not). This point is repeated toward the end of *Sense and Sensibilia*: there is only one sense of "seeing," even if we see different things. If I am looking through a telescope and you ask me what I see, I can answer, quite correctly (1) "A bright speck"; (2) "A star"; (3) "Sirius"; (4) "The image in the fourteenth mirror of the telescope." Austin writes, "I can say, quite correctly and with no ambiguity whatever, that I see any of these."[26] We *see* in a telescope and even in a microscope (and even, according to Hacking, in an acoustic microscope). This point of Austin's could be compared with (and is perhaps an implicit but radical criticism of) Frege, who in "Sense and Reference" uses a similar example (the image in a telescope), playing precisely on the difference between seeing the image and seeing the object.

Seeing is seeing. As Austin says in one of his most remarkable passages: " 'I saw an insignificant-looking man in black trousers.' 'I saw Hitler.' Two different senses of 'saw'? Of course not."[27]

The argument has great philosophical scope; it can be used against not only Ayer's empiricism but also the entire tradition leading up to it, and above all against the theorization of realism after Austin. Indeed there is no sense, for Austin, in saying that we perceive things "indirectly," but neither is there any in maintaining that we see them "directly" (nor in advocating a "direct realism," nor in saying that language has a "direct contact" with things, nor that intentionality refers us "directly" to the world, etc.). *Direct*, like *real*, is a "trouser-word"; that is, a word whose negative version "wears the trousers," to use Austin's analysis—the positive term being defined solely as a function of the negative. The same holds for *real*: "a definite sense attaches to the assertion that something is real, a real such-and-such, only in the light of a specific way in which it might be, or might have been, *not* real."[28] Philosophers must not neglect this point, which is easily brought out by examining uses of *real* and *true* in *Sense and Sensibilia*, chapter 7: "This may save us from saying, for example, or seeming to say that what is not real cream must be a fleeting product of our cerebral process."[29]

We see that Austin's criticism applies in various directions and that on this point as well it is still valid: why should we say that our perception is a product of our brains, or even that it is of the order of intention or representation? What authorizes us to do so? ("But how in fact are we supposed to have been persuaded that sense data are *ever* fleeting products of cerebral processes?")[30] Nothing in ordinary language does, in any case—no more than a foundation for the idea of a conceptualization (or a structuration, since certain philosophers prefer this term, although the difference is not clear to me) of perception can be found in everyday language. In truth, and to repeat, Austin would not say that perception is *not* structured or conceptualized; in this sense, he does not fall for the famous Myth of the Given, so often denounced (and even still, recently, by McDowell). For him the question does not arise. That things appear to us in such or such a way ("look like") is an *ordinary* fact—and this is equally the case in classical examples of illusion, which we all know how to correct. The stick in water does *not* look as if it is bent; it would have to appear quite different for us to think it was. For Austin the submerged stick is only a normal, ordinary case of perception and not an occasion for positing either immateriality or inference: it "is exactly what we expect and what we normally find," and "we should be badly put out if we ever found this not to be so." It is no more an illusion than perspective is, or an image in a mirror or in a movie—once we are familiar with these phenomena. Here, remarkably, it is the *ordinary* that resolves and effaces the question of illusion. "Familiarity, so to speak, takes the edge off illusions" (26). It is as if we were asking whether showing a *photograph* amounts to producing an illusion, "which would plainly be silly."

The appearance of the stick or the photo is merely natural and ordinary, and what we would find abnormal would be if it were otherwise—if the coin looked round and not elliptical, if the moon looked enormous or the stick straight. Here we may think of what Wittgenstein (as quoted by Bouveresse) said to Anscombe regarding the movement of the stars: "Anscombe reports that one time she observed to Wittgenstein that it is easy to understand why the Ancients believed the sun revolved around the earth, since this is indeed the impression it gives. To which Wittgenstein responded by asking what in fact things would look like if appearances suggested instead that the earth revolves around the sun."[31] In this way, Wittgenstein unseated the idea that perception is something like an inference we correct in order to reestablish the truth. (See Bouveresse's analyses of "perception as inference" in chapter 2 of *Langage, perception, et réalité*). Austin expands and radicalizes this remark by showing the absolutely ordinary nature of these classical cases of illusion. There is no reason to consider them deceptive or as cases in which it is necessary to appeal to reasoning or to meanings in order to have the "right" perception. A fortiori, there is no reason (in the most ordinary cases of perception) to assimilate *seeing* to reasoning. Thus, in a sense (and contrary to what philosophers have long said and what cognitivists today maintain), it is not illusion that can better instruct us on the nature of perception, let alone on the "Nature of Reality" as Austin, not without irony, puts it. It is rather an examination of "this little word 'real' "[32] and other words like " 'reality,' 'seems,' 'looks,' etc." (5). If Austin takes issue with Ayer's and other philosophers' theorizations of "real," "true," or "directly," it is because of the contempt they show for ordinary language, their way of *abusing* it (in all senses of the word) by carelessly extending its sense in such a way that it loses all its meaning. "One can't abuse ordinary language without paying for it" (15), says Austin sharply (he does not say, as the French translation too politely puts it, "pay the bill").[33]

Gochet writes in the introduction to his French translation of *Sense and Sensibilia*, "It is indeed the facts of perception and not language that interest Austin. But he believes that studying language is one way to access the facts of perception."[34] It is quite relevant to say that Austin is in this sense not a philosopher of language, and rather that he speaks of reality and of the true. "I am not sure importance is important: truth is."[35] But the examination of language is not "a way to access" phenomena: it *is* the examination of facts. In order to understand what Austin wants to do, it is necessary to present in more detail the method that consists in starting from ordinary language, for this method is not a matter of "belief"—it is based on a reason, among other things: language (our language) is not a reflection or form of experience; it is, for Austin, *part* of experience.

CHAPTER SIX

Language as Given

Words, Differences, Agreements

Words are part of the world—not through the miracle of semantics or reference, or through what they talk about, but simply by themselves. Here is Austin's way of resolving the question of language's "relation" to the real: "There must be a stock of symbols. . . . These may be called 'words.' . . . There must also be something other than the words, which the words are to be used to communicate about: this may be called 'the world.' There is no reason why the world should not include the words, in every sense."[1]

Words, says Austin, are typically "medium sized dry goods"—our typical ordinary objects. This formulation resembles Quine's (words as "standard-sized goods found at market"),[2] but there is nothing physicalist about Austin's affirmation here. Words are not objects like others—in fact, no object is "an object like others" for Austin, who is distrustful of general appellations. We *use* words, and what makes words useful objects is their complexity, their refinement as tools—whence the importance of studying them in order to examine the things of this world. "We use words to learn about the things we talk about when we use these words. Or, if this definition seems too naïve, we use words as a means to better understand the totality of the situation in which we find ourselves brought to use words."[3]

It is precisely the closeness in size between words and ordinary objects that makes this claim possible. We know how important the concept of "size" is for Austin: he writes, for example, that before wondering if Truth is a substance, a quality, or a relation, philosophers should "take something more nearly their own size to strain at."[4] This, as Urmson reminds us, was the goal Austin set for his method, as several of his notes indicate:

"Shan't learn everything, so why not do something else? . . . Advantages of slowness and cooperation. Be your size. Small men."[5]

("Be your size"—as when one tells a child, "Act your age" so that he or she will be reasonable.) Austin insists that nothing is new about this technique of examining words and that it has always existed, since Socrates, producing its "slow successes."[6] But he was undoubtedly the first (and the last) to systematically apply such a method (which Urmson describes in detail in the text cited above)—a method based, on the one hand, on the handiness and familiarity of the objects concerned and, on the other hand, on the shared agreement this method brings about at every stage. This last point is essential, and I will return to it in greater detail later, with regard to Wittgenstein.

Of course, Austin was also not the first to look for a ground for agreement that would allow philosophy a new starting point—this is indeed the entire discourse and claim of philosophy, including logical empiricism. However, it is clear (for Austin at least) that philosophers until the present have failed to find a point of agreement and have lost themselves in interminable and above all, in Austin's opinion, boring discussions. "There is nothing so plain boring as the constant repetition of assertions that are not true, and sometimes not even faintly sensible."[7] Contrary to what is often believed, the problem is not even that philosophers "do not manage to agree" on an opinion or a thesis; the problem is instead managing to agree on a starting point—that is, Austin says, on a *given*. For him, this given is *language*: not as a body of statements or words, but as the place of agreement on *what we should say when*. It is indeed, for him, a matter of an empirical given or, as he sometimes says, experimental data.

> For me, it is essential to come to an agreement from the beginning on the question of "what we should say when." To my mind, experience proves amply that we do come to an agreement on "what we should say when" such or such a thing, though I grant you it is often a long and difficult process. No matter how long it may take, one can nevertheless succeed, and on the basis of this agreement, this given, this established knowledge, we can begin to clear our little part of the garden. I should add that too often this is what is missing in philosophy: a preliminary "datum" on which one might agree at the outset.[8]

This is a response to confusion about the given, about sense data and probably, in a sense, about that much-discussed "realism": Austin adds that agreement (on "what we should say when") is "an agreement on how to determine a certain given," and thus an agreement "on a certain manner, *one* manner, of describing and grasping facts."[9] There is more than *one* way to describe the facts, and this was one of Austin's arguments against a simplistic form of correspondence truth; but if we can "agree on a certain manner of describing facts," we do indeed also discover something. "We do not claim to discover all the truth that exists about everything. We simply discover the facts that those who have used our language for centuries have made the effort to observe, have retained as being note-worthy along the way, and which have been preserved in the course of our language's evolution."[10]

Austin develops this thought (during the same period as the Royaumont Colloquium) in "A Plea for Excuses," an essay that constitutes an explicit manifesto for the method of ordinary language and the agreements this "fieldwork" can elicit and discover. "Here at last we should be able to unfreeze, to loosen up and get going on agreeing about discoveries, however small, and on agreeing about how to reach agreement."[11]

Agreement is possible for two reasons, at least for Austin—Cavell, for his part, considers these insufficiently developed and gives others.

1. Ordinary language cannot claim to be the "last word." "Only remember, it *is* the *first* word"—all that we have available to us. The *anthropological* sense—quite different from the one previously envisioned—of the "fieldwork" Austin proposes derives from claim. The exploration of language is also the exploration of "the inherited experience and acumen of many generations of men."[12] This exploration goes back to Wittgenstein's project for a "natural history" of man.

2. Ordinary language is a compendium of differences, and it "embodies all the distinctions men have found worth drawing . . . in the lifetimes of many generations"; these are certainly more subtle and solid than "any that you or I are likely to think up in our arm-chairs of an afternoon—the most favored alternative method."[13] Here we go beyond the anthropological perspective and enter into another, even more fascinating, of Austin's preoccupations: for it is indeed the capacity to mark differences that makes language such an adequate instrument for expression, and thus it is indeed in language that we must look for the foundation if not of truth, at least of the "true." To cite from the article "Truth": "Further, the world must exhibit (we must observe) similarities and dissimilarities (there could not be the one without the other): *if everything were either absolutely indistinguishable from anything else or completely unlike anything else, there would be nothing to say*" (121).

Here we see in passing that Austin's relation to empiricism is not only critical: the notion of difference establishes the commonality between language and world and makes language a given. Perceiving differences in language allows us to better perceive things. Within this context we can understand the following enigmatic and often-cited passage from "A Plea for Excuses."

> When we examine what we should say when, what words we should use in what situations, we are looking again not *merely* at words (or "meanings" whatever they may be) but also at the realities we use the words to talk about: we are using a sharpened awareness of words to sharpen our perception of, though not as the final arbiter of, the phenomena. For this reason I think it might be better to use, for this way of doing philosophy, some less misleading name than those given above—for instance "linguistic phenomenology," only that is rather a mouthful.[14]

It is this conception of differences and resemblances (a theme he shares with Wittgenstein) that constitutes what might be called Austin's realism; it is a realism that in spite of everything turns out to be a curious form of empiricism: what is given are differences and distinctions, but these do not constitute a prior conceptualization or structuration. (In this sense, one also cannot say that the given is "differentiated"—for Austin, without difference, nothing is given, and "there would be nothing to say.")

It is Cavell who has most clearly brought out the importance of distinctions in Austin and has shown the naturalness of his distinctions, in contrast to those usually established by philosophers:

> Too obviously, Austin *is* continuously concerned to draw distinctions, and the finer the merrier, just as he often explains and justifies what he is doing by praising the virtues of natural distinctions over homemade ones. . . . One of Austin's most furious perceptions is of the slovenliness, the grotesque crudity and fatuousness, of the usual distinctions philosophers have traditionally thrown up. Consequently, one form his investigations take is that of repudiating the distinctions lying around philosophy—dispossessing them, as it were, by showing better ones. And better not merely because finer, but because more solid, having, so to speak, a greater natural weight; appearing normal, even inevitable, when the others are luridly arbitrary; useful where the others seem twisted; real where the others are academic; fruitful where the others stop cold. . . . This is plainly different from their entrance in, say, philosophers like Russell or Broad

or even Moore, whose distinctions do not serve to compare and (as it were) to elicit differences but rather, one could say, to provide labels for differences previously, somehow, noticed.[15]

The *naturalness* of the distinctions traced in language makes them superior to philosophers' distinctions—in particular to the distinctions established through the *analysis* of words. Austin, before Quine, criticized the notion of analyticity and the possibility of establishing equivalences and substitutions between terms. Thus, Cavell writes, also in *Must We Mean What We Say?* "The clarity Austin seeks in philosophy is to be achieved through mapping the fields of consciousness lit by the occasions of a word, not through analyzing or replacing a given word by others. In this sense, philosophy like his is not 'analytical.'"[16]

Austin's philosophy seeks to establish the connection between language and the world not in the traditional analytic terms of realism or correspondence (although there is a sort of rehabilitation of correspondence in Austin's concept of truth), but as a function of *our* adequacy to our words. It will remain for Cavell to show that there is nothing obvious about this adequacy—or rather, that the moments of obviousness in linguistic agreement that give Austin such joy are inseparable from (or are the other side of) an anxiety proper to the use of language and from the risk of radical inadequacy. Thus, Austin's thinking on difference will be able to open the way for a particular form of realism.

Differences are already there, in things as in language—they are not imposed on the given. The remarkable fact that we can agree on these differences *within* language is due to the excellence and fineness of linguistic tools. As Austin says, "Words are our tools, and, as a minimum, we should use clean tools."[17] Pitcher recounts on this subject that Austin did not really like to say that words are "tools," since the word sometimes seems to designate crude instruments. Imagine your impression if, just before passing out on the operating table, you heard the surgeon say, "Ok, I'm going to get my tools." Language is indeed a precision tool. However, there are several advantages to calling language a tool and invoking the notion of usage and utilization that depends on this appellation:

—As Ryle observed, a tool can be used well or misused: "There are rules to keep or break."[18] This is what, for Ryle at least, distinguishes the English "use" from "usage"—usage is a custom that cannot be followed improperly ("misusage" does not exist),[19] whereas "use" is subject to rules that remain for us to discover. It is clear that Wittgenstein would not agree with such a distinction. For Ryle, the possibility of agreement is founded on a certain necessity in usage, and ordinary language philosophy is in fact a normative science. For Austin, agreement suffices in itself (it is a given), and the matter is then to explain and describe it by examining uses.

—The fact that ordinary language is first and foremost a tool is an essential element of its capacity to establish differences. Ordinary language represents the experience and acumen we inherit, but "that acumen has been concentrated primarily upon the practical business of life. If a distinction works well for practical purposes in ordinary life (no mean feat, for even ordinary life is full of hard cases), then there is sure to be something in it, it will not mark nothing."[20] Austin's argument concerning the practical dimension of language would be banally pragmatic if it were not modified by his innovative and radical analysis of practice and action.

The differences Austin establishes most often bear precisely on (different) sorts of action, which in philosophy tend to be all too easily grouped together under a single name, or separated simplistically (for example by distinguishing free and unfree actions). Austin classifies actions in "Excuses," and in the short and remarkable essay "Three Ways of Spilling Ink," he sums up his method by distinguishing between "intentionally," "deliberately," and "on purpose":

> We must . . . imagine some cases . . . and try to reach agreement upon what we should in fact say concerning them. If we can reach this agreement, we shall have some *data* ("experimental" data, in fact), which we can then go on to *explain* . . . by using such methods as those of "Agreement" and "Difference." . . . Of course, we shall then have arrived at nothing more than an account of certain ordinary "concepts" employed by English speakers: but also at no less a thing. And it is not so little. These concepts will have evolved over a long time: that is, they will have faced the test of practical use, of continual hard cases better than their vanished rivals.[21]

Austin's "naturalist" tone and his evolutionary model are not (well, not only) ironic. His understanding joins up with and radicalizes what we have already discovered in Quine and Wittgenstein:[22] language is part of our natural history; it is immanent to it in the strict sense and evolves with it. It is in this sense that Wittgenstein speaks of agreement *in* judgments. And it is in this sense that theories of immanent truth and of internal (or direct) realism approach the problem the wrong way, whereas, Wittgenstein would say, the solution was at our feet, in front of us. It is clear that for Austin (although he never formulates things this way) language makes it possible to talk about the real (to speak truly) because it is *immanent to this real* (and not the other way around). It is not that words are part of things or that they are material objects (Austin recognizes that this is not the case "except in their own little corner"),[23] but rather they are part of the world, or if one prefers, part of our form of life, which is as real as our objects. Here we can see the proximity between Austin and Wittgenstein, which goes far beyond their defense of ordinary language. This is also one of Cavell's central points in *The Claim of Reason*.

We have not finished with empiricism, or with the idea of a given.[24] Perhaps the principal flaw of recent criticism of the given—whether it takes the form of realism, antirealism, or good old idealism—and of most of the discussions surrounding realism is that they are founded on an alternative that is a *petitio principii*: between an indeterminate, formless, "mute" given (which would be nothing) and a structured, conceptualized, sophisticated[25] given (which would no longer be a given). This alternative structures the entire discourse on realism, which I have shown can be fundamentally called into question.

But it is possible that this alternative, and the whole debate, rests on a shared presupposition: the idea that the empirical given is always insufficient (we are not given enough)—as if this insufficiency were part of the definition of the given or of experience. This idea is also present in conceptions according to which the given itself is "theory-laden," conceptualized, or prestructured. In this sense, it is shared by all the current positions on realism. Here one can detect another dogma (another one!), not exactly *of empiricism* (for it is not certain that Hume succumbed to it, even though it was probably born with Hume and out of interpretations of his work), but rather of contemporary empiricists, and obviously of Quine first of all: the idea, which is absolutely central to all recent epistemology, that experience gives us little and that we, thanks to the conjoined miracles of theory, evolution, or our "cognitive capacities," draw a great deal from it. Thus Quine speaks of the contrast between infinitesimal inputs—a few surface irritations—and the result, which is considerable: "meager input and torrential output."[26] Why is this idea always accepted without discussion? What makes it possible to say that experience gives us "little," or less than what we obtain from it in the form of a finished product? Obviously I will not be trying to answer such a question, nor is it certain that the question is even meaningful—but then, the "diminishing" of the given does not have much meaning either. It is clear by now, I hope, that Austin would have been quite perplexed (for all sorts of reasons, philosophical and de facto) by such a claim about the poverty of experience and the richness of our conceptual productions, and that for him if the study of ordinary language can teach us anything, it is quite the opposite: the quantity and variety of what is given to us, its resemblances and differences, in language *and* in the world—if we understand that these are one and the same thing.

Hence, for Austin, the difficulty and above all the absurdity of "reducing" the given to "signs" (or to use Wittgenstein's terminology, "external" symptoms). This is the theme he takes up in "Other Minds"[27] with regard to the idea formulated by J. Wisdom (which in "Truth" is described as downright "inept") according to which we have "all the signs of bread" when we look in the pantry and see it, taste it, and so on.[28] Austin remarks: "Doing these things is not finding (some) signs of bread at all: the taste or feel of bread is not a sign or symptom of bread at all. What I might be taken to mean if I announced that I had found signs of bread in the larder seems rather doubtful, since bread is not normally casketed (or if in the bin, leaves no trace) and not being a transeunt event (impending bread, etc.), does not have any normally accepted 'signs' " (106–7).

The difficulty with most empiricist approaches—and in general with what Cavell, in *The Claim of Reason*, calls "traditional epistemology"—is the shift regularly made from "normal" uncertainty about whether there is real bread there (as opposed to poisoned bread, as Hume suggested), a real goldfinch, an authentic Louis XV sideboard, and so forth, to the question of knowing whether I have before me reality or only its "signs."[29] "If it turns out not to be bread after all, we might say 'It tasted like bread, but actually it was only bread-substitute,' or 'It exhibited many of the characteristic features of bread, but differed in important respects: it was only a synthetic imitation.' "[30]

There is nothing unreal or nonreal about fake bread, or fake sugar (see the discussion of "real cream" in *Sense and Sensibilia*). This well-known argument of Austin's now appears in a new light and perhaps makes it possible to raise doubt about most of the philosophical approaches that claim to examine our "perception" and the "signs" of reality we are dealing with (such is the goal often announced), thinking that in this way one could examine or determine a "natural language of perception," in the absence of nature, which is recognized as definitively inaccessible or in any case not meaningful. For Austin, such an attempt, whether it takes on a metaphysical or naturalist form, amounts not only to an abuse of ordinary language, but above all to an absurdity—the idea that the senses speak, or signify. Contrary to appearances, nothing is more foreign to Austin than this idea that the senses say something. (In this regard, let us note that to translate the title *Sense and Sensibilia* as "the language of perception," as the French translators did, is perhaps a bit deceptive: there is *no* language of perception, nor, undoubtedly, is there even an ordinary language that "talks about" perception.) The idea that the senses speak means that

> Sensa, that is things, colors, noises and the rest, speak or are labeled by nature, so that I can literally *say* what (that which) I *see*: it pipes up, or I read it off. It is as if sensa were *literally* to "announce themselves" or to "identify themselves," in the way we indicate when we say "It presently identified itself as a particularly fine white rhinoceros." But surely this is only a manner of speaking, a reflexive idiom in which the French, for example, indulge more freely than the English: sensa are dumb, and only previous experience enables *us* to identify them. If we choose to say that they "identify themselves" . . . then it must be admitted that they share the birthright of all speakers, that of speaking unclearly and untruly.[31]

The importance of Austin's position here, which is also developed in *Sense and Sensibilia*, has never been sufficiently appreciated. "In fact, of course, our senses are dumb . . . our senses do not *tell* us anything, true or false."[32] His point has been somewhat forgotten, or has been considered outmoded or naive in current theories of perception,[33] but it seems obvious to me that such forgetting is symptomatic and reveals the *scholastic* nature (to use Austin's expression) of many discussions of perception and (so-called) realism today.[34] Perhaps as a result of trying to purify and improve empiricism and do away with its dogmas, the *truth* of empiricism has been forgotten, and the very nature of language along with it. Thus, Austin's final remark in the passage cited is not just a witticism. To believe that there is a language or meaning of sensation—whether it is called "natural" or imposed makes *no* difference in the end—is to misunderstand both the nature of experience and the "nature of language": the fact that language is not only true or false but, as Austin reminds us in "Truth," confused, inadequate, misplaced, and so on. It is also in such remarks that Austin, while calling into question the classic scheme of "correspondence," also manages to define the language-reality connection, which is not so much a connection (once again, a deceptive image) as a mutual understanding and, as Cavell says, a "reciprocal interiority of words and world."[35]

We may also wonder whether the term *correspondence*, and a fortiori *adequacy*—which is obviously a loaded term in philosophy—is indeed ultimately appropriate for what Austin means. For him, "true" designates only one of the possible ways to express the relationship between language and the world ("words-world" again), to express "fitting the facts." "Fitting" designates for him a concept of adequacy that is no longer correspondence, exactitude, or even correctness, but rather the appropriateness or propriety of a statement in certain circumstances, whether it "goes" or not; whether "the collimator," to use Lacan's word, functions or not. "There are various *degrees and dimensions* of success in making statements: the statements fit the facts always more or less loosely, in different ways on different occasions for different intents and purposes."[36]

This new sense of "true" is not at all relativist. Austin's analysis of truth continues in *How to Do Things with Words*, where he looks at the true within the context of the definition of performatives, in order to generalize his conception of constative statements. "True" designates a general dimension of being proper—it is what is appropriate or opportune in certain circumstances. "It is essential to realize that 'true' and 'false,' like 'free' and 'unfree,' do not stand for anything simple at all; but only for a general dimension of being a right or proper thing to say as opposed to a wrong thing, in these circumstances."[37]

Once again a comparison can be made with Wittgenstein: such an understanding of the true as "fitting," as "what works" or is appropriate is also found in the second Wittgenstein with regard to certain relations of adequacy between words and things, situations, experiences, which cannot be thought of in terms of correspondence (logical or mental). This is what we mean by statements like "that's the right expression," or "the word that fits" (*treffend, passend*) for describing a certain thing or situation—a word we search for but do not necessarily find, although we know with absolute certainty when we have found it: "Got it!" Wittgenstein writes, "Just think of the expression (and the meaning of the expression) 'mot juste' (*das treffende Wort*)."[38]

It is a matter of a feeling of "adequacy," which for Wittgenstein is essential to understanding meaning—as when one feels that a proper noun suits, *goes* with a person or thing. "I feel as if the name 'Schubert' fitted Schubert's work and Schubert's face."[39] The vocabulary Wittgenstein uses to describe this feeling is not easily translated: "*Es stimmt*," "Dies *Wort passt, dies nicht*" (218–19). These formulations by Wittgenstein and Austin have nothing to do with a "pragmatist" (in the superficial sense) understanding of truth. Austin specifies that there is a great difference between his conception of truth and pragmatist doctrines: "This doctrine is quite different from much that the pragmatists have said, to the effect that the true is what works, etc."[40] The appropriateness that Austin's doctrine and Wittgenstein's reflections seek to grasp is determined by precise and enumerable—*logical*—criteria that cannot be summed up by the success or effect of discourse, nor by what "works"; quite to the contrary. Thus they have nothing to do with what is commonly understood by pragmatism or a pragmatic conception of truth. This is the whole difference between the verbs *work* and *fit*—the flux of what "works"—and the rigor of adjustment. It is this very rigor that makes it possible to define Austin and Wittgenstein's particular kind of realism, within this adequacy of "fitting the facts," of what "goes"—goes in the sense in which one article of clothing goes with another, not in the sense of a function being performed. Far from any mythology (or aesthetic) of what "is shown" or "suggested" or "revealed," this concept of meaning—without which, according to Wittgenstein, we are blind not only to certain uses but to the entirety of what language *means*—defines the adequacy of words to world and the different ways we have of looking for this adequacy: the "reciprocal interiority" Cavell speaks of, continuing the project of "linguistic phenomenology" that Austin ironically proposed in "A Plea for Excuses."

But the question is no longer the given, or even empiricism or realism, but, from here on, to understand how Austin—and, as well shall see, Wittgenstein—can justify such an inclusion of language, of *what we say when*, within the given; this inclusion is indispensable to the redefinition of the given that I have put forth. It is the question, thus, of how the examination of ordinary language acquires its legitimacy and how in the end it can help us understand what we mean through, or *in* language—how we *mean what we say*.

CHAPTER SEVEN

The Ordinary as Heritage

Natural and Conventional

To return to ordinary language is not to shut oneself up in language—
it is to return to things themselves, so to speak, once the illusion that
a description of our sensations is possible or even meaningful has been
dispelled. In this regard, Austin is much more radical in his rejection of
a certain form of phenomenology than other theoreticians of perception, past and present (from Ayer and Russell to the cognitivists or neo-
Fregeans of today), who seem obsessed with criticizing phenomenology
while at the same time falling into all of its errors. When Austin speaks of
"linguistic phenomenology," he is thinking less of what the philosophy of
language should or could be than of what phenomenology should be (if
there is any sense in saying this): the description of what is there, at our
disposal, and the differences this makes. Here, Austin is simply extending
Wittgenstein's central and obsessive preoccupation. What is given, and is
all that we have, is our common language, our ordinary utterances. This is
the point of Austin's or Wittgenstein's arguments against the idea of primi-
tive or "incorrigible" statements, or statements of "pure experience." The
objection is not that there is (contrary to a certain epistemological discourse, for example) always some theory or some language within experience; it has nothing to do with, for example, Quine's criticism of the notion
of synthetic statements and "protocol" statements. Rather, the objection
is that if there are "primary" statements, or in any case statements that we
do not doubt (or that we consider it "absurd" or "inept" to doubt), these
are not statements of experience or perception or even (to use one of
Quine's categories) of observation, but *ordinary* statements.

In this respect, the logical empiricism of the first half of the twentieth century and the sophisticated and "naturalized" empiricism of the second half are in the same boat, and we may wonder whether Austin or Wittgenstein would really have considered the second a distinct improvement over the first (it is true that, for different reasons, neither of them believed strongly in the idea of philosophy making progress). The problem is not that experience is always mixed with language or convention. Austin, moreover, was one of the first to call into question the division between analytic and synthetic statements, beginning in 1940 when he presented "The Meaning of a Word."[1] The problem is that our statements of experience (no matter what their nature) are not primary at all, and one can no more establish the primacy of statements of experience or perception than of the famous "analytic" statements Quine examined. As Austin writes in "Other Minds," I am as (or even more) certain of things like "the election took place today" (how do you know? "I read it in the *Times*") or "IG Farben collaborated in the war" ("I was on the investigating committee")[2] as I am of statements like "I see a goldfinch" or a "red spot in front of me." This is obviously a position that can be brought together with what Wittgenstein says in *On Certainty*, for example, about statements like "I know I have two hands" or "I know that Napoleon existed," and which is on many points analogous to what Austin says in "Other Minds" about our usage of "I know" or "I am sure." It is quite interesting to look to *On Certainty* and to Bouveresse's commentary on it in chapter 5 of *Le mythe de l'intériorité* for an understanding of the scope of Austin's arguments.[3] Of course, we know that the contact between Wittgenstein and Austin was minimal (Cavell even recounts that Austin pronounced Wittgenstein's name "Weetgenstine"), and we can hardly invoke any mutual influence. However, it seems clear to me that, once one tries to understand the foundation of "ordinary language philosophy," they constitute a unit; we cannot understand the force of their respective philosophical positions without examining this common ground.

It is furthermore remarkable to see how, before Cavell, the double influence of Wittgenstein and Austin acted on someone whose explicit project was to define a "linguistic philosophy": Friedrich Waismann. In one of his last texts, Waismann investigates the senses of "to know." While maintaining a certain disagreement with Austin about the importance of the *uses* of expressions like "I know,"[4] and especially about their so-called performative value (it is true that this is a problematic point in Austin's theory), he presents an altogether radical analysis that is ultimately more interesting than the analysis of "I know" as performative and which comes closer to Austin's positions in *Sense and Sensibilia*:

So long as one is talking in general terms, everyone, of course, agrees that anyone might "just be mistaken." But turn to a concrete situation, and everything is changed. If a man is married, it *just makes no sense* to talk of the possibility of his being mistaken. Possibility indeed! Eye-wash, that is what it is. And so in this case before us: all the philosophers' talk cannot in the least shake the fact that I know this as definitely as anything *can* be known. Every one of you knows hundreds of facts about which there is not the least doubt—facts such as that he is married, what his name is, etc. What, a mistake? *What is certain* if these things are not? They are, in a very real sense, the *prototype* of all certainty....

In this sense, then, there are particular concrete statements which are true beyond doubt, "incorrigible." (But they are very different from those mostly put forward as candidates, e.g. "Here is something red." To be married has, under the proper circumstances, much more claim to being indubitable than "sense-datum statements.")[5]

Here the comparison with Austin imposes itself (and not only because of their shared obsession with the theme of marriage): "If I don't know this, I don't know what it means 'to know'"; but we must also think of Wittgenstein: what defines certainty, knowing, is shared "forms of life," more than "contents" or definitions. Or, to return to my previous analysis: these ordinary, everyday facts (being married, etc.) constitute our given and are as much a part of it as, for example, sense data. We can now see more clearly the meaning of Austin's "rehabilitation" of facts, which is inseparable from the entire ordinary language method. Waismann was also one of the first to produce an extremely developed analysis of action and will (in his remarkable essay *Wille und motiv*),[6] starting from an examination of ordinary language, constantly asking "What would we say about someone who says," and rising up against the "violence done to ordinary language" by classical philosophical theories of action and freedom. As we shall see, this is also a subject dear to Austin, and it seems that reflection on action and on the connection between language and action is central to ordinary language philosophy—not only because, as is usually thought, "saying is doing," but also because our different ways of talking about what we do are *real* differences between our ways of doing things, and thus the connection between word and action must be conceived in a much stronger and more realistic manner than a superficial examination of the theory of performatives would seem to imply. In short, here again, to talk about language is not the same as doing philosophy of language, and we may, along with Cavell, wonder if there is still any sense in saying that Wittgenstein or Austin do philosophy of language:

Whether the thoughts he produces should be called a "philosophy of language"
depends on what it is one expects from a philosophy of language. Wittgenstein
has some fairly definite ideas about meaning and understanding and signs and
communication and propositions and uses of words; and these are topics a philosophy of language, on any account, is likely to discuss. But Wittgenstein's interest in them is no more nor less than his interest in the topics of intention and
willing and thinking and belief and privacy and doubt and teaching and pain
and pity and conviction and certainty. They are topics in which the soul interests
and manifests itself, so the soul's investigation of itself, in person or in others,
will have to investigate those topics and those interests as and where they ordinarily manifest themselves.[7]

But this is exactly what so often displeases philosophers in both the
Continental and the analytic traditions about ordinary language philosophy: that it claims to speak about philosophical questions (and not just
about language), that it applies what are felt to be arbitrary ordinary uses
to such fundamental questions. I have already examined certain of Austin's justifications for this method—they are perhaps not sufficient, and we
must still examine, with the help of Wittgenstein and Cavell, the reasons
for this claim.

What is the method that starts from ordinary language based on? Precisely on nothing—nothing other than our ordinary usages, our language,
inherited from others, from the *majores homines* evoked at the beginning
of the *Philosophical Investigations*. This is the point that I have always
sought to emphasize with regard to what is known as "the second Wittgenstein": the radical immanence of our life in language. There is *nothing else* in language besides the inheritance I have come into by learning
different usages. "Our ordinary language . . . pervades all our life."[8] This
sense of the immanence of language led me to bring together the conceptions of language learning in Quine and in Wittgenstein: learning creates
a linguistic community around a "core" of firmly accepted statements. In
other words, what defines a linguistic community is its members' adher-
ence to certain statements (this is what made it possible to redefine analyticity). The following passage from the *Philosophical Investigations* comes
to mind: "If language is to be a means of communication there must be
agreement not only in definitions but also (queer as this may sound) in
judgments. This seems to abolish logic, but does not do so."[9]

In Quine, what founds logic is the capacity of a community to "agree
in" statements or judgments; to assent to them because, in fact, belonging

to the community is based on this assent. Cavell remarks on this subject: "It is not necessary that we should recognize anything as 'logical inference'; but if we do, then only certain procedures will count as drawing such inferences, ones (say) which achieve the universality of agreement, the teachability, and the individual conviction, of the forms of inference we accept as logic. . . . The fact is, those who understand (i.e., can talk logic together) do agree. And the fact is that they agree the *way* they agree; I mean, the ways they have of agreeing at *each* point, each *step*."[10]

In my interpretation of Quine, logic was thus conceived of as *obvious* in the sense that within our linguistic community logical truths meet with universal assent and because, inversely, assent to these truths defines belonging, *assent*, to a community of speakers. This communitarian interpretation of the status of logical truths was based essentially on a reading of Wittgenstein, but also on a certain interpretation of behaviorism. Behaviorism "means something"—a structure shared by Quine and Wittgenstein that we may once again describe as *anthropological*: a child, by definition, cannot speak at birth. She or he has only the language of others available—not her or his own. Wittgenstein stated this clearly in the *Investigations*, spelling out the implications of Augustine's thinking: "And now, I think, we can say: Augustine describes the learning of human language as if the child came into a strange country and did not understand the language of the country; that is, as if it already had a language, only not this one."[11] Children learn *all* their language from others; language is an inheritance—thus, Wittgenstein defines language learning at the beginning of the *Investigations* as "training" (*Abrichten*). This definition can produce an analysis of the status of both logical and moral norms in terms of learning and acceptance by the community. The example from the *Brown Book* is well known: a child in a tribe where language is reduced to a few words is taught to count to twenty and to continue if one makes a certain gesture. Wittgenstein specifies: "If a child does not respond to the suggestive gesture, it is separated from the others and treated as a lunatic."[12] For Wittgenstein, this means that adaptation and learning coincide: adapting to the world and to society implies learning a language, and learning a language can take place only through and within the integration of a social norm. In learning a language, one learns norms. In Quine, because "language is a social art,"[13] it is the art of transmitting norms. This normative and regulative aspect of learning a language was, in the end, one of the most profound points—*the* anthropological point—of Quine's work. It was this anthropological radicalness that seemed to justify Quine's frequently

expressed lack of interest in the examination of linguistic usages. But in
reality, the significance of this philosophical point appears more clearly
once we attempt to further define the idea of anthropology and of "form
of life." On the basis of such an examination, it turns out to be impossible
to make naturalism à la Quine (the origin of current forms of naturalism) and naturalism à la Wittgenstein (a reflection on "what is natural
to us") hold together. Symmetrically, it turns out to be difficult, in spite
of some interesting proximities, to make conceptions of *convention* like
Quine's (which can be shown, in "Truth by Convention" in particular and
in Quine's relationship to Carnap in general,[14] to fit squarely within the
tradition of Carnap's conception) cohabit with Wittgenstein's (who effects
a radical transformation of the idea of convention in the *Philosophical
Investigations*). Instead of attempting such futile balancing acts or turning anthropology into a vague buzzword that would make it possible to
resolve every philosophical problem, it is necessary to go back to the very
foundation of the anthropological approach: our shared agreement on or
rather *in* language—and, more specifically, the *we* in question in "what
we say when." We always return to the same questions: What grounds the
appeal to ordinary language? By what right do we refer to "our usages"?
And who is this "we"?

As I have said repeatedly, all we have is what we say, our agreements in
language. This is what led Quine, quite lucidly, to define Austin's approach
as the search for "introspection" rendered objective through recourse to
a "group" technique,[15] which he curiously compares to the radical translator's approach (which also proceeds by applying an initially individual
given to the elements of a community). However, it appears difficult to
interpret the linguistic agreement Wittgenstein speaks of and to which
Austin appeals in terms of strategies of translation or interpretation.
Austin's skepticism about meanings is even more radical than Quine's (for
example, in Austin's text "The Meaning of a Word"):[16] we do not agree
on meanings, but on usages, as Wittgenstein also saw clearly. We determine "the meaning of a (given) word" through its usages, and for Austin,
to ask the question of meaning differently (in general, or by looking for
an entity) is "nonsense." The search for agreement (asking "what would
you say if . . . ," as Austin does constantly) is based on something entirely
different from meanings or the determination (even if problematic and
underdetermined) of common sense. The agreement Austin speaks of is
not at all an intersubjective agreement, and it is not based on a "convention" or on actual agreements made between civilized speakers. In this

sense, it has nothing to do with the "solidarity" that Rorty, for example, speaks of. It is as objective an agreement as possible (Austin spoke of "experimental data"), and it bears as much on language as on reality. But what is this agreement? Where does it come from, and why accord it such scope and weight? This is Cavell's question, beginning in the first essays of *Must We Mean What We Say?* and later, more fully, in *The Claim of Reason*. In all his work, Cavell poses the same question: what allows Austin and Wittgenstein to *say what they say about what we say?* Where do they get all this? The answer is rich with surprises and paradoxes. Cavell first discovered a radical absence of foundation to the claim to "say what we say," and then—a further discovery—that this absence is not the mark of any lack of logical rigor or rational certainty in the procedure that begins from this claim. This is the meaning of what Wittgenstein says about our "agreement in judgments" and in language: it is based only on itself, on *us*. Obviously there is material for skepticism here, and this is indeed the main subject of *The Claim of Reason*. But to understand the nature of our language and our agreements is also to recognize that this "does not abolish logic"; to the contrary, it represents something fundamental about our rationality—what Cavell defines as, in the strict sense, *the truth* of skepticism. *The Claim of Reason* is, in its entirety, an elaboration on a remark Cavell made in "The Availability of Wittgenstein's Later Philosophy," which served as the introduction to his doctoral thesis, "The Claim to Rationality," out of which came the book *The Claim to Reason*. The remark is a simple reading of Wittgenstein, but it finds in him a discovery, perhaps anthropological, which, like many of Wittgenstein's discoveries, is "simple and difficult" at the same time.

> We learn and we teach certain words in certain contexts, and then we are expected, and expect others, to be able to project them into further contexts. Nothing insures that this projection will take place (in particular, not the grasping of universals nor the grasping of books of rules), just as nothing insures that we will make, and understand, the same projections. That on the whole we do is a matter of our sharing routes of interest and feeling, modes of response, senses of humor and of significance and of fulfillment, of what is outrageous, of what is similar to what else, what a rebuke, what forgiveness, of when an utterance is an assertion, when an appeal, when an explanation—all the whirl of organism Wittgenstein calls "forms of life." Human speech and activity, sanity and community, rest upon nothing more, but nothing less, than this. It is a vision as simple as it is difficult, and as difficult as it is (and because it is) terrifying.[17]

I have quoted this long passage in order to show the shift Cavell makes from the question of common language to the question of a community of forms of life—a community that is not just the sharing of social structures, but of everything that constitutes the fabric of human existences and activities. It is for this reason that sociological interpretations and uses of Wittgenstein always miss the real sense of his "anthropology": for him, it is not enough to say, "This is how we do it." The problem is connecting the *I* to the *we* and vice versa. In this way, skepticism is inherent to all human practice: whether linguistic or other, it makes little difference, since all certainty or confidence in what we do (continuing a series, counting, etc.) is modeled on the certainty and confidence we have in our shared usages of language.

McDowell comments on this passage of Cavell's:

> The terror of which Cavell speaks at the end of this marvelous passage is a sort of vertigo, induced by the thought that there is nothing but shared forms of life to keep us, as it were, on the rails. We are inclined to think that this is an insufficient foundation for a conviction that when we, say, extend a number series, we really are, at each stage, doing the same thing as before. In this mood, it seems to us that what Cavell describes cannot be *a shared conceptual framework* within which something is, given the circumstances, objectively the correct move.[18]

As McDowell tries to show in his work on Wittgenstein, this disquiet (this vertigo) derives from an illusory understanding of deductive certainty, which is no more (or less) grounded than the other activities Wittgenstein describes, and vice versa: if we accept the idea that practices like counting, and so forth, are immanent to our forms of life (dependent on them, says McDowell), and yet rational, there is all the more reason to believe our other practices are. According to McDowell, we thus have the "treatment" for this vertigo: immanent acceptance of our dependence. It has indeed been well demonstrated by authors like Bouveresse, Diamond, and McDowell that for Wittgenstein this meant reconceiving the rationality at work in activities like mathematics. But it does not follow as obviously as McDowell makes out that the question of skepticism then disappears. "The acceptance of forms of life," immanence, is not a ready-made answer to philosophical questions, and Wittgenstein surely would not have appreciated a certain contemporary discourse, inspired by his work, in which an appeal to "the acceptance of forms of life" becomes a refusal to investigate or question these forms and a pretext for talk of the end of philosophy. All of Rorty's reading and exploitation of Wittgenstein is clearly guided by such a "conformist" interpretation of the notion of form of life.[19] From this point of view, one of the great merits of Cavell's reading—whether or not one appreciates its tragic dimension—is his altogether radical questioning of such an understanding of forms of life, a questioning that turns out to be inseparable from maintaining and transforming the skeptical question. Cavell shows *both* the fragility and the depth of our agreements and focuses on the very nature of the necessities that for Wittgenstein emerge from our forms of life. The significance of Cavell's work for the philosophy of language can, for me, be summarized in the following three important points:

1. As McDowell says, there is rationality and objectivity to the procedures based in our "forms of life." This is indeed what Cavell has always said, since *Must We Mean What We Say?* and it also means that necessity of usage is inherent to *all* our uses of language, from the moment we *mean* something. A rule is thus neither a foundation nor an explanation: it is *there*, which in no way diminishes its rigorous—because "natural"—character. A particularity of Cavell's position is his redefinition of the necessity of usage and of the rules of language in terms of *nature*: for him this very particular naturalism defines the *ordinary*.

2. For Cavell, thus, no "treatment" for skepticism emerges out of the fragility of our agreements. That our ordinary language is based on nothing other than itself is a source of disquiet not only about the validity of what we do and say: it is the revelation of a truth about ourselves that we do not wish to recognize—the fact that "I" am the only possible source of such validity. To reject this, to attempt to erase skepticism, amounts to reinforcing it. This is what Cavell means by his famous proposition that skepticism is lived. This is not an "existential" interpretation of Wittgenstein but a new understanding of the fact that language is our form of *life*.

3. The acceptance of this fact, which Cavell defines as "the absence of foundation or guarantee for finitude, for creatures endowed with language and subject to its powers and impotences, subject to their mortal condition," is thus no consolation here, no deliverance, but rather the "acknowledgement" of finitude and of the everyday, whose source Cavell finds in Emerson and Thoreau, founders of the thought of the ordinary. It is on this condition that we can again find the "lost contact with reality," the proximity to the world and to words broken in skepticism. Thus, the often discussed answer to the question of realism can be found only

in ordinary language, within what Austin and Wittgenstein show to be the imbrication, the "reciprocal interiority" of language and life. The adequacy of language to the world—the truth of language—is not to be known or demonstrated: it is shown, as we have begun to see with Austin, *in* language. (This is an idea I am also drawing from the form of realism Diamond defends in *The Realistic Spirit*).

Cavell's originality lies in his reinvention of the nature of language and in the connection he establishes between this nature and *human nature*—finitude. It is for this reason that the question of agreements in language reformulates ad infinitum the question of the human condition and that acceptance of the latter goes hand in hand with recognition of the former. What is at stake, then, for Cavell, is the acceptance of *expression* itself: to tolerate being expressive, to tolerate meaning. In this way the question of meaning is reformulated: meaning is no longer sense or denotation but, as Wittgenstein's English terminology at the beginning of the *Blue Book* indicates, mean*ing*.

CHAPTER EIGHT

The Myth of Inexpressiveness

The philosophical problem raised by ordinary language philosophy seems double. First, by what right do we base ourselves on what we ordinarily say? Second: on what, or on whom, do we base ourselves in order to determine what we ordinarily say? But—and this is the genius of Cavell's line of questioning in *Must We Mean What We Say?* and in *The Claim of Reason*—these two questions are but one: the question of the relationship between me (my words) and the real (our world); that is, for Cavell as for Wittgenstein, the question of our *criteria*. To see this, let us go back to the examination of agreements in language. These agreements determine and are determined by criteria: We share criteria by means of which we regulate our application of concepts and through which we establish the conditions of conversation. In the *Investigations*, Wittgenstein searches for and determines our criteria, which govern what we say. But *who is he*, asks Cavell, to claim to know such things? It is the absence of foundation for the claim to know what we say that underlies the idea of criteria and defines the term *claim*. "The philosophical appeal to what we say, and the search for our criteria on the basis of which we say what we say, are claims to community. And the claim to community is always a search for the basis upon which it can or has been established. I have nothing more to go on than my conviction, my sense that I make sense. . . . The wish and search for community are the wish and search for reason."[1]

The central enigma of rationality and community is thus how it is possible for me to speak *in the name of others*. But this is exactly the problem in "Other Minds": knowing how to access the minds of others, which was also Wittgenstein's obsession:

How does [Wittgenstein] know such things? I mean, apart from any philosophical claim into whose service he would press such findings, how can he so much
as have the idea that these fleets of his own consciousness, which is obviously
all he's got to go on, are accurate wakes of our own? But the fact is, he does
have the idea; and he is not the only one who does. And the fact is, so much of
what he shows to be true of his consciousness is true of ours (of mine). This is
perhaps the fact of his writing to be most impressed by; it may be the fact he is
most impressed by—that what he does can be done at all.[2]

This explains the very particular tone of the *Investigations*, which have
something autobiographical about them—but a curious autobiography,
which would be our own as well. "It can seem sometimes that Wittgenstein
has undertaken to voice our secrets, secrets we did not know were known,
or did not know we shared. And then, whether he is right or wrong in a
given instance, the very intention, or presumption, will seem to some out-
rageous."[3] This tone of confidence brings Wittgenstein close to Rousseau
and Thoreau, for example, and it led Cavell to discover, within the reflection on language agreements that emerges out of the *Philosophical Investigations*, a radical investigation of the nature of subjectivity: "The writer
has secrets to tell which can only be told to strangers. The secrets are not
his, and they are not the confidences of others. They are secrets because
few are anxious to know them; all but one or two wish to remain foreign.
Only those who recognize themselves as strangers can be told them, because those who think themselves familiars will think they have already
heard what the writer is saying. They will not understand his speaking in
confidence."[4]

There is, then, no refutation of skepticism by the ordinary in Wittgenstein. Such a refutation would in any case be circular, for the ordinary is
precisely what is threatened by skepticism. But above all, for Wittgenstein
as for Austin, there is nothing immediate or obvious about the ordinary:
it must be discovered, and this discovery is the task Austin sets for himself
in his meticulous analyses, and Wittgenstein in his innumerable examples.
What I mean to say, once more, is that the appeal to ordinary language is
not at all a facile solution to philosophical problems, and it most certainly
cannot be reduced to a return to good sense or common sense. This is
what separates Wittgenstein and Austin most sharply from a philosopher
like Moore (regardless of his influence and the fascination he held for
many; see Bouveresse's analyses in *Le mythe de l'intériorité*).[5] The examples Austin and Wittgenstein give have nothing in common with Moore's

type of argument—for example, his argument against the philosophical thesis that there are no material objects: "You are certainly wrong, for here's one hand and here's another; and so there are at least two material things"; or against the thesis that time does not exist: "If you mean that no event ever follows or precedes another event, you are certainly wrong; for *after* lunch I went for a walk, and after that I took a bath, and after that I had tea"; or that there are no sensations other than my own: "I know that *you* now see me and hear me, and furthermore I know that my wife has a toothache, and therefore it follows that sensations, feelings, experiences other than my own exist."[6] These arguments can be criticized not for their bluntness or simplicity, but because they share the same problematic as the thesis they are trying to refute, and in this way they reinforce it.

Moreover, thinkers like Moore (and, to a lesser degree, Russell and Ryle) always seem to know what our common sense is from the outset, what we say or think ordinarily. But there is nothing more difficult or painful to know: Austin goes to great lengths to discover what we mean by "intentionally" or "It is a fact"; Wittgenstein needs all of the *Investigations* just to find out a little better whether we think we have access to the minds of others. In *The Claim of Reason*, Cavell never ceases investigating our *ordinary* manner of conceiving the suffering of others, or the relation of the soul to the body: why, for example, is it easier for us to imagine the soul of a prince in the body of a frog than the soul of a frog dressed as a prince? Do we ordinarily conceive of the soul, the "I," as *in* my body, or as being my body? Of course, these are questions to which there is no immediate answer, and the ordinary, far from being a solution to skepticism, is, to the contrary, shot through with it. This brings us back again to the question of the ground of agreement: the question of the nature of the *I, my* capacity to speak, and thus to conform to shared criteria. It is not enough to invoke the community; we still do not know what authorizes me (entitles me) to refer to it, to consider myself a full-fledged member of it.

> When I remarked that the philosophical search for our criteria is a search for community, I was in effect answering the second question I uncovered in the face of the claim to speak for "the group"—the question, namely, about how I could have been party to the establishing of criteria if I do not recognize that I have and do not know what they are. . . . [The answer must] emphasize that the claim is not that one can tell a priori who is implicated by me, because one point of the particular kind of investigation Wittgenstein calls grammatical is exactly to discover who.[7]

We may, in this vein, continue to examine the notion of convention, which up to now I have done from a Quinean perspective. Indeed, Cavell allows us to investigate "what are commonly known as linguistic conventions." The strength of his analysis of conventions in chapter 5 of *The Claim of Reason*—and what sets it apart from Rorty's analysis of community and convention—is that it brings out the deeply problematic nature of any appeal to convention, and in particular the absurdity of talking about "conventionalism" in Wittgenstein. This is revealed in the quote from the *Philosophical Investigations* that serves as a guiding thread for all of Cavell's work:

> —It is what human beings *say* that is true and false; and they agree in the *language* they use [*in der Sprache stimmen die Menschen überein*]. This is not agreement in opinion but in forms of life.
>
> If language is to be a means of communication there must be agreement [*Übereinstimmung*] not only in definitions but also (queer as this may sound) in judgments. This seems to abolish logic but does not do so.[8]

That we agree *in* language is certainly not the end of the problem of skepticism, and conventionalism is not an answer to the questions posed here. In fact, for Cavell it is crucial that Wittgenstein says we agree *in* and not *on* language. This means that we are not the agents of the agreement, that language as much precedes this agreement as it is produced by it, and that this circularity itself constitutes an irreducible element of skepticism. An answer to the question of language will not be found in convention, because convention is not an *explanation* of the functioning of language but rather a difficulty and a mystery. Most conventionalist interpreters of Wittgenstein (I am of course thinking here of Kripke) go down a false path: the idea of convention, especially if it is conceived in a "conventionalist" manner, so to speak, will not help us define agreement in language. The idea of convention does indeed mean something (in this sense, we cannot get around it): it recognizes the strength of our agreements and the extraordinary character of our capacity to speak together. But it cannot explain the real practice of language, and it is used instead to avoid seeing the *naturalness* of language. As Cavell says: "Since we cannot assume that the words we are given have their meaning by nature, we are led to assume they take it from convention; and yet no current idea of 'convention' could seem to do the work that words do—there would have to be, we could say, too many conventions in play, one for each shade of each word in each context. We *cannot* have agreed beforehand to all that would be necessary."[9]

Agreeing *in* language means that language—our form of life—produces our accord as much as it is the product of an agreement; that in this sense it is natural to us, and that the idea of convention is there both to mimic and mask its necessity: "Underlying the tyranny of convention is the tyranny of nature," Cavell said.[10] Here Cavell's criticism, in *This New Yet Unapproachable America*, of the usual interpretations of "form of life" enters.[11] He uses the expression forms of *life* (and not *forms* of life): it is our forms of *life* that are given. The refusal of this given, of the form of life in both its social and biological dimension, is what leads us to want to break our agreements, our criteria. Cavell insists on this second ("vertical") aspect of form of life, while at the same time recognizing the importance of the first ("horizontal") aspect, social agreement. The endless discussions of the first sense (conventionalism) have occluded the force of the natural sense of the form of *life* in Wittgenstein—the sort of *fatality* of the ordinary, which Wittgenstein delineates by evoking "natural reactions" and "the natural history of humanity." What is given in forms of life is made up not only of social structures and various cultural habits but of everything that has to do with "the specific strength and scale of the human body, senses and voice" (41–42); everything that makes it such that like Kant's dove, which needs air to fly, we need friction in order to walk.[12] With the idea of convention, the naturalness of language—which is, contrary to appearances, as essential or even more essential to its *publicness* as is its conventionality—is forgotten or repressed: "It is a wonderful step towards understanding the abutment of language and the world when we see it to be a matter of convention. But this idea, like every other, endangers as it releases the imagination. For some will then suppose that a private meaning is not more arbitrary that one arrived at publicly, and that since language inevitably changes, there is no reason not to change it arbitrarily. Here we need to remind ourselves that ordinary language is natural language, and that its changing is natural."[13]

It is precisely by perceiving the naturalness of language that we can get back to language's natural realism. Conventionalism, with its insistence on the arbitrariness of language and the conventionality of the relationship of words to the world, distances us from this natural realism. (It is thus no great surprise that the most conventionalist interpretations of Wittgenstein inevitably drag him toward a sophisticated form of antirealism, even idealism, not to mention Rorty's relativism). Calling into question the concept of convention allows us to redefine a new form of naturalism, which no longer has much to do with the naturalism professed today by those who adhere to the cognitive sciences, and which is nevertheless rooted in facts of nature much more certain, or in any case, much more difficult to deny: exactly what Wittgenstein meant by our "form of life."

At the end of the first part of *The Claim of Reason* (in a passage that has become quite famous and which inspired, notably, Putnam's title *Words and Life*), Cavell explores what he calls "the natural ground of our conventions":

> What is the natural ground of our conventions, to what are they in service? It is inconvenient to question a convention; that makes it unserviceable, it no longer allows me to proceed as a matter of course; the paths of action, the paths of words, are blocked. "To imagine a language means to imagine a form of life" (cf. §19). In philosophizing, I have to bring my own language and life into imagination. What I require is a convening of my culture's criteria, in order to confront them with my words and life as I pursue them and as I may imagine them; and at the same time to confront my words and life as I pursue them with the life my culture's words may imagine for me: to confront the culture with itself, along the lines in which it meets in me.[14]

This leads Cavell to redefine the task of philosophy in terms often taken up in recent American philosophy: philosophy is "the education of grownups":

> In this light, philosophy becomes the education of grownups. It is as though it must seek perspective upon a natural fact which is all but inevitably misinterpreted—that at an early point in a life the normal body reaches its full strength and height. Why do we take it that because we then must put away childish things, we must put away the prospect of growth and the memory of childhood? The anxiety in teaching, in serious communication, is that I myself require education. And for grownups this is not natural growth, but *change*. Conversion is a turning of our natural reactions, so it is symbolized as rebirth.[15]

The recourse (return) to the ordinary and to ordinary uses of language is thus a way of carrying out this change. It is, however, clear that this transformation cannot be thought of as an answer to skepticism: it is rather the recognition of the *truth of skepticism*, articulated several times by Emerson: "I know that the world I converse with in the city and in the farms, is not the world I *think*. I observe that difference and shall observe it. One day, I shall know the value and law of this discrepance. But I have not found that much was gained by manipular attempts to realize the world of thought."[16]

This is the justification for Cavell's shift from the problematic of ordinary language to the problematic of transcendentalism, which is the problematic of the ordinary *tout court* but *defined by language*. The ordinary, moreover, is also a myth or an illusion, as Cavell affirms in a striking passage: "Wittgenstein's appeal or approach to the everyday finds the (actual) everyday to be as pervasive a scene of illusion and trance and artificiality (of need) as Plato or Rousseau or Marx or Thoreau had found. His philosophy of the (eventual) everyday is the proposal of a practice that takes on, takes upon itself, precisely (I do not say exclusively) that scene of illusion and loss."[17]

As Cavell discovered after *The Claim of Reason* with his (re)discovery of Thoreau and Emerson, what remains to be shown is the idea of an intimacy, a proximity with the world that in his later writings appears fatally problematic: "[the idea] that Austin's and Wittgenstein's attacks on philosophy, and on skepticism in particular—in appealing to what they call the ordinary or everyday use of words—are counting on some intimacy between language and world that they were never able satisfactorily to give an account of.[18]

Cavell constantly reminds us that this proximity was also Kant's problem—the problem of the possible or necessary adequacy of our understanding to the world. And in Cavell's reading of Wittgenstein, Austin, and Kant, the problem cannot be solved if it is posed in philosophical terms, for a radical reason: the impossibility of *grounding* the relation of my language to the world (this is what Cavell calls the truth of skepticism). But perhaps the best way to pose the problem is not in terms of foundation, nor in terms of intersubjectivity or objectivity, but by analyzing the very demand for foundation. As in certain enigmas, the solution may lie in the form of the question, where one would not have expected it (as Cora Diamond suggests in *The Realistic Spirit*). Thus, by examining "the claim of Reason" to express or explain its own adequacy to the world (which, let us recall, was also the subject and enigma of the *Tractatus Logico-Philosophicus*), it will be possible to shed light on, if not answer, the question of skepticism—and thereby, I hope, to better understand the question of realism. The Kantian inflection of the notion of "claim" indicates Cavell's wish to inscribe the *Investigations* within the continuation of the *Critique*'s transcendental investigation (and of the *Tractatus*'s as well, which is more easily done). When Wittgenstein says that his investigation is "grammatical" and specifies that it "is directed [*richtet sich*] not towards phenomena, but, as one might say, towards the '*possibilities*' of phenomena,"[19] for Cavell this indicates that "what he means by grammar, or a grammatical investigation, plays the role of a transcendental deduction of human concepts." The difference with Kant lies in that, for Wittgenstein, every word of our ordinary language requires a deduction; "each is to be tracked, in its application to the world, in terms of what he calls criteria that govern it." It is in this sense that our grammar is to be understood as a priori: in the sense that "human beings are 'in agreement' in their judgments."[20] For Cavell, another return to the Kantian question can be found in transcendentalism, which resolves the loss of "intimacy of words with the world"[21]—as Thoreau does in *Walden*, for example—through the ordinary observation that "the universe constantly and obediently answers to our conceptions."[22] This leads Cavell to read the philosophy of ordinary language and the transcendentalism of Emerson and Thoreau as "reactions" to skepticism and, more specifically, as continuations of "the Kantian insight that Reason dictates what we mean by a world."[23] For Cavell, the question of how words "hook onto" the world is translated by the word *claim*.

Here is a first approach to the sense of claim: it is the pretension to speak for "us," a claim at once curious and legitimate, as is, for Kant, the claim of reason to ask questions that are outside its power. We may here recall the epigraph to the second part of *The Claim of Reason*, which is taken from the preface to the first edition of the *Critique of Pure Reason*: "Human reason has this peculiar fate that in one species of its knowledge it is burdened by questions which, as prescribed by the very nature of reason itself, it is not able to ignore, but which, as transcending all its powers, it is also not able to answer."[24]

Cavell inscribes this tension, which in Kant is proper to human reason (and which is exactly expressed by the word *claim*: a pretension that knows it is in a sense impossible to satisfy), within the usage of language. But as the title of Cavell's book indicates, in going from reason to language, nothing has changed. The naturalness of reason—questions are "prescribed by the very nature of reason itself"—just like that of language, is impossible to push away and impossible to bear, or to satisfy. This is what guides the definition of the sense or senses of *claim* in Cavell. We have already seen that *claim* signifies my pretension to speak in the name of the community, but its meaning is not only linguistic. Wittgenstein's criteria pose a question that is equally *political* and philosophical. This is not only the question of my belonging to the community of those who speak my language, but also the question of my representativeness: from where does the right to represent come to me? What grounds it, philosophically? "The criteria

Wittgenstein appeals to—those which are, for him, the data of philoso-phy—are always 'ours,' the 'group' which forms his 'authority' is always, apparently, the human group as such, the human being generally. When I voice them, I do so, or take myself to do so, as a member of that group, a representative human."[25]

But I am not representative of the human "by definition." The agree-ment can always be broken. I can be excluded (or exclude myself) from the community, either linguistic or political. The possibility of disagreement is inherent to the very idea of agreement, from the moment I claim (through my words) my representativeness. This ever-possible disagreement sums up the threat of skepticism: the break in the passage and suspension of the generalization from the *I* to the *we*. "Two questions are immediately to be expected: (1) How can I, what gives me the right to, speak for the group of which I am a member? How have I gained that remarkable privilege? What confidence am I to place in a generalization from what I say to what everybody says?: the sample is irresponsibly, preposterously small. (2) If I am supposed to have been party to the criteria we have established, how can I fail to know what these are?"[26]

For Cavell, the question of the social contract underlies or defines the question of language agreements, as his analysis of Rousseau at the begin-ning of *The Claim of Reason* shows. If I am representative, I must have my voice in the common conversation. If my society is my expression, it must also allow me to find my voice. But is this really the case? As Cavell subsequently showed in *Conditions Handsome and Unhandsome*, it is not at all obvious. This is the illusion or mask that he denounces in Rawls and his *Theory of Justice*. What makes it possible to say that in the "original position" I consented to society and, to thus summarize Rawls's stance, that I consent to it at present? If others stifle my voice or speak for me, I will always seem to consent. In chapter 3 of *Conditions Handsome and Unhandsome*, Cavell seeks to call into question the *entirety* of Rawls's ap-proach and its very spirit as well as his conception of justice, by contrasting it with Emersonian perfectionism.[27] Can one speak of justice, of contract, or of agreement if one forgets that some are cast off, rejected, and lack a voice in the "conversation of justice"? Such is the political analysis one can develop of the notion of "voice" as it emerges from *The Claim of Reason*. If others stifle my voice or speak in my place, I will always seem to consent. It is not by nature that you have a voice, *a voice of your own*: it must be found in order for you to speak in the name of others and in order to let them speak in your name. This shows the proximity of the question of contract—the *political* question in general—to the question of learning. Because if others do not accept my words, I lose more than language: I lose my own voice. "We do not know in advance what the content of our mutual acceptance is, how far we may be in agreement. I do not know in advance how deep my agreement with myself is, how far responsibility for the language may run. But if I am to have my own voice in it, I must be speaking for others and allow them to speak for me. The alternative to speaking for myself representatively (for *someone* else's consent) is not: speaking for myself privately. The alternative is having nothing to say, being voiceless, not even mute" (28).

The error of post-Wittgensteinian scholasticism is to see the private-public duality as a strict alternative (this is the prejudice underlying the interminable discussions of "the private language argument"). Cavell explodes this alternative. To not be public is not to be *private*: it is to be *inexpressive*. Voiceless. If I do not speak, it is not that there is something inexpressible, but that I *have* nothing to say.

Our agreement (with others, with ourselves) is an agreement of *voices*: our *übereinstimmen*, says Wittgenstein. "That a group of human beings *stimmen* in their language *überein* says, so to speak, that they are mutually voiced with respect to it, mutually *attuned* top to bottom,"[28] writes Cavell. In this way, Cavell defines an agreement that is *not* psychological or intersubjective and which is based purely on the validity of a voice: my individual voice claims to be, is, a "universal voice." *Claim* is what a voice does when it bases itself on nothing other than itself (and thereby on its agreement with itself) in order to establish universal assent: a claim that, as exorbitant as it already is, Cavell asks us to formulate in an even more exorbitant manner: that is, in place of and instead of any condition of reason or understanding. Reason itself is both the object and the subject of "claim" (and this is the meaning of the ambiguity of the genitive in the title *The Claim of Reason*).

In *Must We Mean What We Say?* Cavell posed the question of the foundation of language in the Kantian terms of "universal voice," showing the proximity between Wittgenstein's and Austin's methods and a paradox inherent in aesthetic judgment: basing myself on *me* in order to say what *we* say. This is how we may think of the type of rationality that creates and defines the philosophy of ordinary language: "I will suggest that the aesthetic judgment models the sort of claim entered by these philosophers, and that the familiar lack of conclusiveness in aesthetic argument, rather than showing up an irrationality, shows the kind of rationality it has, and needs."[29]

Cavell begins with an analysis of Hume in order to show that if *agreement* produces judgments of taste, this does not mean it is irrational. This is also the meaning of *claim*: the discovery of a sense of rationality that is not exhausted by the concept of scientific rationality. "Hume's descendants . . . have found that aesthetic (and moral and political) judgments lack something: the arguments that support them are not conclusive the way arguments in logic are, nor rational the way arguments in science are. Indeed, they are not. . . . It does not follow, however, that such judgments are not conclusive and rational."[30]

Kant develops this idea in §8 of *The Critique of Judgment*, which could perhaps turn out to be the source for thinking about agreement here. With aesthetic judgment, Kant leads us to discover "a property of our faculty of cognition that without this analysis would have remained unknown": the "claim to universality" proper to judgments of taste, which makes us "[ascribe] the satisfaction in an object *to everyone*."[31] Kant then distinguishes the agreeable from the beautiful (which claims universal agreement) in terms of *private* versus *public* judgment. How can a judgment with all the characteristics of a private judgment claim to be public, valid for all? Kant noted the strange, "disconcerting" nature of this fact, whose strangeness Wittgenstein took to the limit. The judgment of taste demands universal agreement, and it "does in fact expect [such assent, *Einstimmung*] of everyone."[32] It is what Kant calls the universal voice (*allgemeine Stimme*) that supports such a claim. This voice, *Stimme*, is heard in the idea of agreement: *übereinstimmen*, the verb Wittgenstein uses when speaking of our agreement in language.[33] It is the universal voice that postulates our agreement, and thus our claim, to speak in the name of others—that is, to speak at all. "Kant's 'universal voice' is, with perhaps a slight shift of accent, what we hear recorded in the philosopher's claims about 'what we say': such claims are at least as close to what Kant calls aesthetical judgments as they are to ordinary empirical hypotheses. . . . I wish to suggest that it is a claim or dependence of the same kind."[34]

It is for these reasons as well that the question "What do we say ordinarily?" is not "only" a question of language but, as Austin always asserted, a question that bears (on) things themselves. In *Must We Mean What We Say?* Cavell, bringing together Austin and Wittgenstein with regard to this point, noted: "One sometimes has the feeling that Austin's differences penetrate the phenomena they record—a feeling from within which the traditional philosopher will be the one who seems to be talking about mere words."[35] "Such facts perhaps only amount to saying that the philosophy of ordinary language is not about language, anyway not in any sense in which it is not also about the world. Ordinary language philosophy is about whatever ordinary language is about" (95).

Familiarity with and proximity to things (which I have gradually defined here as the naturalness of language) certainly constitute the center of (ordinary) language—its (our) claim to things insofar as they are spoken (what Austin called doing things with words): this is exactly the demand included under the title of "claim." The claims of ordinary language philosophy thus consist in demanding that one listen to language and that one do what the philosophy of language (in its various recent forms— semantic, pragmatic, or cognitivist) has given up on doing by repressing the dimension of Austin and Wittgenstein's work that insists that language is always also a *voice*.

> Kant's attention to the "universal voice" expressed in aesthetic judgment seems to me, finally, to afford some explanation of that air of dogmatism which claims about what "we" say seem to carry for critics of ordinary language procedures, and which they find repugnant and intolerant. I think that air of dogmatism is indeed present in such claims; but if that is intolerant, that is because tolerance could only mean, as in liberals it often does, that the kind of claim in question is not taken seriously. It is, after all, a claim about *our lives*.[36]

In spite of their differences, both Austin and Wittgenstein tried to render explicit that language is part of our lives—this is what can be called their realism. As Montefiore and Williams remark, "The facts to which both Austin and Wittgenstein wished to recall philosophy were very commonplace and everyday facts of ordinary life . . . just facts of the common world, shared with the least philosophical human observer."[37]

To bring words back "from their metaphysical to their everyday use," back to the shared ordinary, as Wittgenstein always sought to do, is not to do "philosophy of language": it is to come closer to the real. In order to conclude, we must still determine the sense of this proximity.

CHAPTER NINE

To Speak, To Say Nothing, To Mean to Say

U p to now, I have not insisted on the differences that separate Austin and Wittgenstein.[1] In fact, what interests me here is what they have in common—a form of realism that one hardly dares call realism, since it is precisely what is forgotten or rejected by philosophy today—analytic or otherwise—and in the debates over realism.[2] Truth to tell, the difficulties in ordinary language philosophy's reception are not new, and Cavell's first texts, which appeared at the beginning of the sixties, showed particularly well the accumulated misunderstandings of Wittgenstein's work and, to a lesser degree, of Austin's. When, in *Must We Mean What We Say?* (chapter 3, "Aesthetic Problems in Modern Philosophy"), Cavell specifies the rational dimension of aesthetic statements, for example, he goes against the dominant theory of the time, *emotivism* (also called noncognitivism)—a doctrine that, as MacIntyre's works have shown,[3] still plays a determining role in thought today. This doctrine derives from the idea that only cognitive statements, which represent "states of affairs," are veritable statements endowed with "meaning," and other statements therefore cannot express anything except an emotive attitude regarding such statements. One origin of this idea can be found in the "descriptive" scheme according to which language is primarily intended to speak of states of affairs. I have shown that this scheme—called representationalist and which, in *Phénoménologies et langues formulaires*, Claude Imbert attributes to the concept of an "apophantic pact"[4]—is presented in typical fashion in Wittgenstein's *Tractatus*. The world is the totality of facts (states of things) (1.1), we make a picture (*Bild*) of facts (2.1), more specifically, a logical picture, which is thought (3). Thoughts are meaningful propositions (*der sinnvolle Satz*) (4), the only ones about which we can ask whether they are true or false. There can thus be no ethical propositions (6.42). "There is indeed the inexpressible. This *shows* itself" (6.522; see also 4.1212, "what *can* be shown *cannot* be said").[5] Several conclusions can be drawn from this rapidly sketched structure: what cannot be said is *sinnlos*, but it can be shown. On this point, it is necessary to bring in Diamond's and Bouveresse's remarkable analyses of the notion of non-sense. First, the distinction between *saying* and *showing* does not mean that what is shown is shown *outside of language*. What is shown is shown *in* language. Next, there are no statements that would say nothing yet would vaguely show something, an inexpressible content: a statement without meaning *doesn't mean anything*, it does not try to say something that cannot be said.[6] As Diamond says regarding Frege (but the point is valid for Wittgenstein as well), there are no thoughts without meaning: "There are vague sentences, and there are individual people who think, as it were, in fuzzes, who fail to entertain any definite thought. But *the* mind has no fuzzes and no logically confused thoughts." There are not, on the one hand, confused thoughts to be improved and, on the other hand, rigorous thoughts. Nonsense *is* nonsense: "There is no nonsensical thought expressed by a nonsensical sentence."[7] Wittgenstein says in the *Investigations*: "When a sentence is called senseless, it is not as it were its sense that is senseless."[8] Thus, Diamond shows that the brilliance of Frege's *Begriffsschrift* (and the aspect of its structure that Wittgenstein wanted to maintain in the *Tractatus*) is that in it thought is defined entirely by logic and "the way logic and mathematics penetrate *all* thought is shown in the notation . . . itself"[9] (this is a point she finds formulated in Geach, in the parallel he establishes in his article "Saying and Showing in Frege and Wittgenstein").[10] This idea that everything is shown *in* language, not somewhere else outside of language, is what Wittgenstein means in the *Tractatus Logico-Philosophicus*.

There is thus a deep misunderstanding (which was the starting point of my reflection on Austin) in the use that has been made of the *Tractatus* to exclude a certain category of statements—whether philosophical, logical, or ethical-aesthetic—from the field of language. The *Tractatus*'s definitions (the proposition as state of affairs) have been interpreted as criteria of meaning and have been used to introduce criteria of empirical meaning, with the result that ethical or aesthetic statements, for example, have no meaning. A statement is devoid of meaning (if we follow Carnap in "The Elimination of Metaphysics," a text typical of this approach) when it cannot be verified or checked empirically. This does not prevent Carnap from saying that what lacks meaning in language can be expressed by artists, musicians, and so on: hence—and here is the difference from Wittgenstein—outside of language. True or false applies only to sentences that express a state of affairs, or, in the more empiricist version, sentences that can be reconstructed in terms of experience and logic—in short, sentences with cognitive content. In his postface to the French translation of *How to Do Things with Words*, François Récanati argues that beginning in the twenties, analytic philosophy gradually tried to "legitimize" nonsense.[11] Thus, he finds in Ogden and Richards's famous 1923 book, *The Meaning of Meaning*, which was a first version of the "emotive theory of language," an outline of ordinary language philosophy. Language is no longer envisioned solely in its cognitive dimension, in what it says, but in what it *means*. Certain statements do not describe a state of affairs; they express a "sentiment" (emotion) in relation to a state of affairs. Certainly, as Récanati rightly points out, "with the emotive theory of ethics, the domain of the non-cognitive regained all the dignity it had lost."[12] But there was a price to pay: this domain is both excluded from language (since it is nondiscursive) and "scientifically" recoverable within the framework of psychological explanation—which most certainly leads us quite far from the perspective on nonsense opened by Wittgenstein.

Contrary to the vulgate interpretation of the *Tractatus* popularized by Ogden and Richards, and in a different way by the Vienna Circle, nothing is more false for Wittgenstein than the idea that the aesthetic cannot be spoken or belongs to the "emotive" domain—and, more generally, as Cavell has said, that there would be a division in language between a cognitive capacity and a noncognitive capacity: between one part of language whose function would be to "respond" to reality and another part that would not have to do so.[13] Such an assertion might seem curious, given that this division came directly out of discussions of the *Tractatus* and its famous distinction between saying and showing. But for this Wittgensteinian distinction, we must think of Frege, and not Carnap or Ayer. On this point, I refer to Geach's text on saying/doing, which I have already mentioned and which was also Diamond's starting point.[14] After drawing a remarkable parallel between Frege and Wittgenstein, Geach asserts that one unanswered question from the *Tractatus* is where, in what "place," what these ethical propositions show is shown—whereas there is (once we have read Geach, Diamond, or Bouveresse, in any case) an obvious answer to the question of where what logical propositions show is shown: in language (which language remains to be seen, and here the question of the shift from the first to the second Wittgenstein comes in). "The Frege-Wittgenstein notion of what comes out but cannot be asserted is almost irresistible, in spite of its paradoxical nature, when we reflect upon logic. Wittgenstein's view is that superficially indicative statements of ethics, aesthetics, and religion must be assigned the same role as the strictly improper sentences used didactically in logic: the role of conveying insights. The difficulty besetting this further view is that it is a much more obscure question how we can tell in these cases that an insight actually has been conveyed."[15]

In this article, Geach concludes that there is no solution to this enormous problem within Wittgenstein's work itself.[16] Now, an examination of Wittgenstein's second philosophy could lead to partially weakening that conclusion (and I believe this is one goal of Cora Diamond's work): the answer to the question of where ethical or aesthetic statements show themselves is the same as the answer to where logical statements do: in language. But it remains to be seen how, and for this, Austin's theories can help us as much as the *Philosophical Investigations*.

Austin was the first to have affirmed clearly that all our ordinary statements have a relation to what is true. It is often thought that the result of Austin's work on speech acts is the elimination of the criterion of truth for performatives and thus, generalizing his theory, for all statements. The reality, as Cavell has recently reminded us, is exactly the opposite: Austin does indeed want to destroy what he calls "1) the true-false fetish and 2) the value-fact fetish,"[17] but destroying them does not mean abandoning the concept or criterion of truth; it means enlarging it, extending it outside of the domain of "description." " 'False' is not necessarily used of statements only," Austin says at the end of the first lecture in *How to Do Things with Words* (11). The argument for the end of the "T/F fetish" (for which Quine criticized Austin) is not a relativist argument;[18] rather, it reintroduces necessity into a domain of ordinary language that seemed to lack it. In the same way, in Wittgenstein—contrary to certain interpretations—the notion of a rule is not a substitute for truth but an extension of truth to statements where truth does not seem valid. Neither Austin nor Wittgenstein rejects the notion of truth: to the contrary, they extend the criterion of adequacy to reality to all ordinary statements. Here again, Austin's procedure is radical: he applies the notions of true/false and even, conversely, of felicity/infelicity and success/failure (which were initially defined as proper to performatives) to all statements.

It is well known that at first Austin did indeed propose to replace the true/false duo with felicity/infelicity in the case of performatives: a performative (for example, a promise) is infelicitous, failed, if it is carried out in inadequate conditions, which Austin describes and classifies (for example, if I do not intend to keep my promise, or am not entitled to carry out the act). Of course, one of Austin's ideas is to destroy "1) the true-false fetish and 2) the value-fact fetish." But as we saw in detail in "Truth," he does not eliminate truth but rather modifies the philosophical conception of it. "The truth or falsity of a statement depends not merely on the meanings of words but on what act you were performing in what circumstances."[19]

This extremely clear conclusion from the eleventh lecture of *How to Do Things with Words* shows that Austin, far from wanting to renounce truth, wants to redefine its meaning or rather, here, its domain. "'False' is not necessarily used of statements only," Austin writes at the end of the first lecture in *How to Do Things with Words*: for him it is not a matter of abandoning the criterion of truth for a certain category of statements, nor of defining its conditions outside of language, but rather of redefining truth by retracing the limits of language, of *what can be said*. To show this, I quote from his twelfth lecture.

> In particular, the following morals are among those I wanted to suggest:
>
> (A) The total speech act in the total speech situation is the *only actual* phenomenon which, in the last resort, we are engaged in elucidating.
>
> (B) Stating, describing, etc. are *just two* names among a very great many for illocutionary acts; they have no unique position.
>
> (C) In particular, they have no unique position over the matter of being related to facts in a unique way called being true or false, because truth and falsity are (except by an artificial abstraction which is always possible and legitimate for certain purposes) not names for relations, qualities, or what not, but for a dimension of assessment.[20]

This is the meaning of the invention of speech acts, which at bottom has nothing to do with pragmatism, and this meaning can be seen clearly only within the framework of the entirety of Austin's work. If speech acts exist, and if (as Austin showed in his lectures) every statement is also a speech act, then language is no longer solely descriptive or representative: "In saying something we do something, or even *by* saying something we do something."[21] Inversely, truth extends to statements that are not only descriptive; truth no longer exactly affirms a "correspondence," or a "representation," but instead is something like an adequacy to the facts. We may thus speak of *truth* for (apparently) performative statements. As Austin said in "Truth": "It is common for quite ordinary statements to have a performatory 'aspect': to say that you are a cuckold may be to insult you, but it is also and at the same time to make a statement which is true or false."[22]

It is, furthermore, the essay "Truth" that can help us understand the stakes of *How to Do Things with Words*. In this essay, Austin envisioned the different modes of a statement's adequacy to facts, in this way criticizing the *Tractatus*'s semantics and picture theory. Can an image be "true"? "If a map can be clear or accurate or misleading, like a statement, why can it not be true or exaggerated? . . . These are the really illuminating questions."[23] A theory of the true should be able to explain other types of success or failure of statements: not only the true and the false, but also the vague, the rough, the adequate or the out of place, the relevant or the inept (130). But all these evaluations are as rigorous and codified as those of truth. This is what Austin shows in, for example, "A Plea for Excuses."

For a performative utterance to be successful, conditions of truth are necessary ("I promise" and "Excuse me" are not true or false in the sense that they describe an act or an inner state; rather, for them to be successful, certain statements must be true—that I keep my promise, for example). If I say "Excuse me" and I am really excusing myself then it is true and not false that I am excusing or have excused myself, that certain conditions have been fulfilled, and that I am bound to a subsequent action. Performatives have their own truth conditions. This appears clearly in Austin's distinction between lying (speaking falsely) and *insincerity*. "The unhappiness here is, though affecting a statement, exactly the same as the unhappiness infecting 'I promise . . .' when I do not intend, do not believe, etc. The insincerity of an assertion is the same as the insincerity of a promise. 'I promise but do not intend' is parallel to 'it is the case but I do not believe it'; to say 'I promise,' without intending, is parallel to saying 'it is the case' without believing."[24]

The examination of *failures* of performatives thus has remarkable consequences: it makes it possible to see how descriptive functions can also "go wrong." This proves that for utterances in general, failure or falsity depend on "the total speech act in the total speech situation." This obviously makes it possible to assimilate so-called constative statements to performatives.[25]

In this way, the invention of the performative reveals the nature of *all* our utterances: constatives are subject to all the infelicities that affect performatives, which finally undoes the performative (felicitous-infelicitous)/ constative (true-false) dichotomy. The strength of Austin's theory is precisely that it is a theory of truth, of language's relationship to the real, without being a theory of representation. It is for this reason that it is completely absurd to consider the theory of speech acts as a detachable and independent element (as is most often done in philosophy of language since Austin, especially in pragmatics): the theory is in fact inseparable from the rest of Austin's philosophy, which implies the final explosion of the performative-constative distinction.

Another altogether curious consequence of Austin's theory is that it calls into question the very concept of action, defined on the model of the performative utterance as that which can fail, turn out badly. It is not only language that Austin calls into question: it is action itself. Austin discovered the pragmatic dimension of language, and the field of pragmatics went in this direction, extending pragmatism and proceeding as if appealing to the notion of action could illuminate language and meaning—as if this notion were primary and obvious. But Austin uses actions not to *explain* the functioning of language, but in order to show a difficulty. To say that we *do* things *with words* is to say that action—all action—is structured like an utterance and that there is something in action that is akin to language. Thus, the great theme of pragmatism to which he refers ironically (the user's-manual title *How to Do Things with Words*, an ironic homage to pragmatism, was chosen by Austin for his William James Lectures) is reversed: far from being the beginning of everything, action becomes as problematic as words.

In order to bring out this point further, we may avail ourselves of one of Austin's little-known theories, his examination of excuses. "A Plea for Excuses"[26] indeed reveals the relation between act and language that remains implicit in *How to Do Things with Words*. The theme of this essay poses exactly the same problem—the relation between action and discourse—that the theme of performatives does, but in a different and inverse form, starting from action this time. Austin, preventing in this way any moralizing recuperation of his theory, notes at the outset that the question of excuses could help us in moral philosophy if we had the slightest idea of "what is included under, and what not, the expression 'doing an action' or 'doing something'" (178). In fact, we do not know. One must not forget that in the background of the theory of performatives is a real perplexity about what it is *to do something* (with or without words). We actually have no idea, and philosophers who contemplate the question fall for the "myth of the verb" according to which there is some "thing," "doing an action," which brings out all the essential characteristics of what we *classify* under the stand-in "doing an action" and which would be common to the most divergent cases, which in this way all become equivalent. "All 'actions' are, as actions (meaning what?), equal, composing a quarrel with striking a match, winning a war with sneezing: worse still, we assimilate them one and all to the supposedly most obvious and easy cases, such as posting letters or moving fingers, just as we assimilate all 'things' to horses or beds" (179).

In reality, excuses—*what we say when* it appears that we have acted poorly (clumsily, inadequately, etc.)—make it possible to better understand what an action is, or rather, to begin to classify what we group together under the general term *action*. The existence of excuses is essential to the nature of human action—they are not somehow added on after the fact but are implicated in this nature. As Cavell says, "What does it betoken about human actions that the reticulated constellation of predicates of excuse is made for them—that they can be done unintentionally, unwillingly, involuntarily, insincerely, unthinkingly, inadvertently, heedlessly, carelessly, under duress, under the influence, out of contempt, out of pity, by mistake, by accident, and so on? . . . It betokens, we might say, the all but unending vulnerability of human action, its openness to the independence of the world and the preoccupation of the mind."[27]

"Excuses," says Cavell, "are as essentially implicated in Austin's view of human action as slips and overdetermination are in Freud's."[28] Excuses bind acts and language together as tightly as performative utterances do, showing what an illusion it would be to "explain" or ground language with acts. Once more, this is what I am interested in: we do not really know what it is to *say* or *mean* something, any more than we know what it is to *do* something.

At the beginning of "A Plea for Excuses," Austin notes: "These are expressions still too little examined on their own account and merits, just as the general notion of 'saying something' is still too lightly passed over in logic. There is indeed a vague and comforting idea in the background that, after all, in the last analysis, doing an action must come down to the making of physical movements with parts of the body; but this is about as true as that saying something must, in the last analysis, come down to making movements of the tongue."[29]

Is saying something an action? Has the problem raised by the existence of performative utterances really been solved by explaining that they are acts? These are the kinds of questions one can ask on the basis of "A Plea for Excuses." The result is once again the imbrication of action and language and, once again, the reciprocal interiority of words and world: what Cavell calls our "openness to the independence of the world." As I have begun to show, to understand language is to see how our words are inextricably mixed in with our life. In my opinion, Austin carried this idea through to the end. It is also to understand something about our *nature*, our subjection to the rules of language, which are far more numerous and constraining than we imagine when we try to ground (through logic, for example) the connection between language and the world. This observation can be taken in two different directions:

1. *It can be taken in the direction of renewing a speaker's relationship to language, his or her "meaning."* In the essay "Must We Mean What We Say?"[30] Cavell already posed the question that obsesses his work: how to *mean* (think, signify) what I say? Here again, Cavell reverses radically the investigation of "private language." The problem is not being able to express what I have "in me," thinking or feeling something without being able to say it: it is the inverse, not being able to *mean what I say*. It is not thought that is beyond or beneath my speech; it is language that surpasses me. In this sense, I am more "possessed" by language than I possess it (and the conventionalist illusion is there to attenuate this reality). This point is expressed in *A Pitch of Philosophy*, where Cavell says that Austin "affirm[s] that I am abandoned to [my words], as to thieves, or conspirators"[31] and makes explicit one of his intuitions about the source of skepticism: the impossibility of speaking the world does not comes from an (imaginary) distance from the world, but rather from the impossibility of or the refusal to *mean*. "What they had not realized was what they were saying, or, what they were *really* saying, and so had not known *what they meant*. To this extent, they had not known themselves, and not known the world."[32]

The question, from this point forward, is no longer being able to access language or the community of speakers, or finding one's voice: it is being able to bear, precisely, "the (inevitable) extension of the voice, which will always escape me and find its way back to me."[33] We are, says Emerson in a gripping passage, "victims of expression."[34] What is unbearable is not the inexpressible, the impossibility of expressing something inner (everything that has to do with the "myth of interiority"); it is expression itself. Out of this unbearableness the fantasy of the private is born, a fantasy that according to Cavell disguises or transforms our fear of being public, of abandoning ourselves to language, into a symmetrical fear of inexpressiveness. "It is in recognizing this abandonment to my words, as if to unfeasible epitaphs, presaging the leave-taking of death, that I know my voice, recognize my words (no different from yours) as mine."[35]

This is exactly the subject of the fourth part of *The Claim of Reason*: the fantasy of privacy, of *inexpressiveness*. "So the fantasy of a private language, underlying the wish to deny the publicness of language, turns out, so far, to be a fantasy, or fear, either of inexpressiveness, one in which I am not merely unknown, but in which I am powerless to make myself known; or one in which what I express is out of my control."[36]

The question of the absence of meaning, of non-sense, is transformed here and becomes the question of meaning: the question of the fatality of meaning, my "condemnation" to signification. The problem is thus no longer exactly non-sense, absence of sense, but rather the fatality of expression.

> The question, within the mood of the fantasy, is: Why do we attach significance to *any* words and deeds, of others or of ourselves? . . . How can anything we say or do count as doodling, be some form of nonsense; and why is all the rest condemned to meaning?
>
> A fantasy of necessary inexpressiveness would solve a simultaneous set of metaphysical problems: it would relieve me of the responsibility for making myself known to others—as though if I were expressive that would mean continuously betraying my experiences, incessantly giving myself away; it would suggest that my responsibility for self-knowledge takes care of itself—as though the fact that others cannot know my (inner) life means that I cannot fail to."[37]

To understand that language is our form of life, as Wittgenstein says, means accepting the naturalness of language, the fatality of meaning. It is not easy to achieve this recognition. It is out of this that skepticism, in all its various forms, is born: the impossibility of accessing the world is a mask for my own refusal to know or acknowledge the world, that is to say, to bear signification, meaning, expression. Out of this, realism, in all its various forms, is also born: my claim to know or theorize the world is a mask for my refusing contact or proximity with things. To recognize the existence of the world and to recognize that we speak it "is equally to acknowledge that your expressions in fact express you, that they are yours, that you are in them. This means allowing yourself to be comprehended, something you can always deny. Not to deny it is, I would like to say, to acknowledge your body, and the body of your expressions, to be yours, you on earth, all there will ever *be* of you."[38]

2. *Another form of the constraint of language on our lives might emerge out of examining psychology's statements.* In criticizing the famous cognitive-emotive distinction in *Must We Mean What We Say?* Cavell did not only want to defend Austin; he was reversing a standard interpretation of the *Tractatus*, as well as of the *Philosophical Investigations.* The domain of nondescriptive ordinary statements—for example, those of psychology or ethics—is, ultimately, *not* exempt from logic. One might think that starting in the thirties, Wittgenstein renounced a logical conception of thought and agreed to study "all of language," including what was notoriously nonsense, the statements of psychology, and so forth—that he started picking through the *Tractatus's* trash bins, in a sense. To think so would be to make yet another error. Wittgenstein changed, but in another respect. He maintained the idea of a nonpsychological treatment of the mind,[39] but the "necessity" that presided over this was no longer logical necessity ("the crystalline purity of logic")[40] but the necessity of rules and our usages. The approach and the direction, however, remain the same: a nonpsychological treatment of the mind insofar as it is entirely *there*—in logic, and now, in the use of language, in our agreements. This change is summed up in a passage in the *Philosophical Investigations* written around 1930, at the moment when Wittgenstein was reexamining certain of the *Tractatus's* theses.

> Here we come to the apparently trivial question, what does Logic understand by a word—is it an ink-mark, a sequence of sounds, is it necessary someone should associate a sense with it, or should have associated one, etc., etc.?—And here, the crudest conception must obviously be the only correct one.
>
> And so I will again talk about "books"; here we have words; if a mark should happen to occur that looks like a word, I say: that's not a word, it only looks like one, it's obviously unintentional. This can only be dealt with from the standpoint of normal common sense. (It's extraordinary that that in itself constitutes a change in perspective.)[41]

The change is a further renunciation, and this is what it really means, as Diamond says in *The Realistic Spirit*, to "push away the ladder." The "prejudice of the crystalline purity" of logic is given up: the idea that logic is the only form of a rule.

> We see that what we call "sentence" and "language" has not the formal unity that I imagined, but is the family of structures more or less related to one

another.—But what becomes of logic now? Its rigour seems to be giving way here.—But in that case doesn't logic altogether disappear?—For how can it lose its rigour? Of course not by our bargaining any of its rigour out of it.—The *preconceived idea* of crystalline purity can only be removed by turning our whole examination round. (One might say: the axis of reference of our examination must be rotated, but about the fixed point of our real need.)[42]

To recognize that usages and the rules of using language are what gives life to signs (and not anything psychical or psychological) does not mean giving up "the rigor of logic" but finding it again, where one least expects to (at least, from the point of view of logic): in our ordinary uses themselves, *in* language: it is there, to finally answer Geach's question, that logic *shows* itself.

> "Everything is already there in . . . " How does it come about that this arrow →
> *points*? Doesn't it seem to carry in it something besides itself?—"No, not the
> dead line on paper; only the psychical thing, the meaning, can do that."—That
> is both true and false. The arrow points only in the application that a living be-
> ing makes of it.
> This pointing is *not* a hocus-pocus which can be performed only by the
> soul.[43]

To say that everything lies in use means, as we have seen in all sorts of ways, that there is nothing else in what we say, and nothing with which to make our language and usages agree. To push away the ladder of the *Tractatus*, for good this time, and as Diamond says, not to "chicken out,"[44] is to understand this. Thus, we see why the perspective of ordinary language and its immanent agreements, if we follow it all the way to the end, is radically antimetaphysical. We could also call it "realistic" (in the sense in which Diamond speaks of the "realistic spirit"). The only agreement to be sought is *in* language—that is, as Kant already said, in a use that agrees with itself: "[Logic] is to teach us the right use of the understanding, that is, its use agreeing with itself [*den mit sich selbst übereinstimmenden Gebrauch*].[45]

All of Frege's thought and the *Tractatus* constitute a response to this Kantian question of a use of the understanding "agreeing with itself [*den mit sich selbst übereinstimmenden Gebrauch*]" and with nothing else, but the *Investigations* do as well: they take up Kant's proposition literally, by affirming that we must look for our agreement in language, the agreement of language with itself *in* our very uses. And Austin's philosophy also does the same (we should recall, at this point, that Austin was a translator of Frege and warned against the excessive sophistication of contemporary interpretations of clear Fregean terms such as *word* or *phrase*):[46] it inscribes the sole possibility of finding an agreement with the world within our agreements—our agreements on *what we say when*—and thus, it redefines *logic within ordinary language*, revealing the real sense of Wittgenstein's famous statement: "—It is what human beings *say* that is true and false; and they agree in the *language* they use. This is not agreement in opinion but in forms of life."[47]

(If one speaks of "agreement on" language, as is usually the case in French translations and in many commentaries, one loses what Wittgenstein is saying here, and the antimetaphysical as well as antipsychological radicalness of his claim. One also loses the obvious proximity with Kant.) Kant's proposition—to be in agreement with oneself—and the *Tractatus*'s—on a necessity that can only be *logical*—are turned around here, while at the same time they are taken up again in exactly the same terms: taken at their word, in a sense, through a clue that, as often in Wittgenstein, leads us to look for the answer where one never would have thought. For the mind to find "a use agreeing with itself," it is necessary precisely to turn to usages, in which we agree (our *übereinstimmen*). It is *in* language that everything necessary for understanding is carried out (and "this does not abolish logic": it is logic itself). This is the form of "agreement with oneself" and with others that the *Philosophical Investigations* discover and carry out, and it is the final step in the "de-psychologization of psychology" that Frege started at the beginning of the century and which Wittgenstein thus completes.

This agreement in usages might sum up the perspective that I have tried to develop. It is not necessary to look any further than our agreement to find the real, but there is nothing obvious about doing this, and patience is needed. Here, perhaps, is a final way of defining realism. And here, once again: "This seems to abolish logic but does not do so."[48]

To the contrary, it is undoubtedly the passage through, or rather *in*, ordinary language that can in the end give us a definition of what logic is, of what is logical (*ce qui est [la] logique*).

Conclusion

If we return for a moment to the debate of the 1960s, we realize that the opposition I evoked at the beginning of this book between two kinds of philosophy of language is perhaps not so clear-cut: the logical analysis of language on the one hand and the philosophy of ordinary language on the other (in an important text, Récanati has distinguished these as the first and second analyses)[1] seem, in the end, to come together in their shared criticism of well-anchored conceptions (notably, the idea that there is a way to match language to the world, or a point of view from which to do so) and in a certain philosophical radicalness. This radicalness might be defined in terms of a rejection of traditional empiricism: as we have seen, it led thinkers as different from one another as Austin and Carnap to reject the idea of "incorrigible" statements. But it might also be defined as the invention of a new sort of empiricism: Austin's goal is indeed to re-define the given and the data of experience in order, as he says at the end of "Ifs and Cans," to open the way for "a true and comprehensive *science of language*." He does not reject the idea of logical syntax, but rather the idea that there is a difference between this logical syntax and the ordinary grammar of our usages. "Do we know, then, that there will prove to be any ultimate boundary between 'logical grammar' and a revised and enlarged *Grammar*?"[2] This rare optimism of Austin's has led some to imagine that later developments in linguistics have carried on his work and have even solved the difficulties raised in his philosophy. This is not the case, and Austin constantly claims, in his way, the *logical* character of his approach. In truth, Austin's work, like that of the second Wittgenstein, fits much better into the framework of the first kind of philosophy of language than is typically believed—even if attention to ordinary language and the project of describing its uses obviously constitute an important new element, the meaning of which I have tried to establish here. One indication of this proximity between Austin and logical empiricism is the double radical-ness—antipsychological and antimetaphysical—of both Vienna Circle and Oxford Circle philosophy; another indication is their will to define a certain type of philosophical *non-sense* and to denounce an illegitimate, twisted, or "wild" use of language by traditional philosophy.

Austin's approach, like that of the second Wittgenstein, can be conceived not as a renunciation of the claims of analysis but as their extension: to show the rigor—the same rigor we attribute to logic—that presides over our uses of language and the workings of our language games: what Wittgenstein called "the hardness of the soft."[3] On this point, we have followed Cora Diamond's analyses. Wittgenstein himself recognized in a note, "The style of my sentences is extraordinarily strongly influenced by Frege," and he said this influence could be seen "where at first sight no one would see it."[4] I believe it is possible to show a continuity between the first analytic philosophy and linguistic philosophy—against the tendency of many current presentations of the matter, which in one way or another exaggerate or mythicize the difference between analytic philosophy as defined by Frege, the *Tractatus*, and Carnap on the one hand and analytic philosophy as practiced by Austin and Wittgenstein beginning in the 1930s on the other hand—whether in order to overrate the first moment and deplore the descent or degeneration into ordinary language, or to vaunt the merits of a Wittgensteinian turn that would destroy analytic philosophy and its prejudices. In fact, these two attitudes are completely equivalent and reinforce each other. What I would like to oppose to them—and this is the project I have presented here—is a new reading of ordinary language philosophy that would define the force, or the necessity, of the rules of our common usages within their immanence: as the very necessity of both the linguistic given and logic.

This new reading is the extension or continuation of the procedure showing the continuity between the two moments of the philosophy of language, and it is a pursuit of *realism*, in a renewed sense: a realism of the rightness [*justesse*] of our uses of language and the differentiations they make (or discover; it is the same thing, if we understand what "difference" means. As Austin says, if one makes a distinction, it is because there is one. This is, if you like, his realism). Thus, in a thinker like Austin there is a will to understand fully the idea, formulated by Carnap and destroyed by Quine and then Davidson, that the questions of philosophy are questions of language, and to understand that this is a realist idea. For my part,

I have insisted greatly on Quine's criticism of meaning and on a certain point of view shared by Quine, Austin, and Wittgenstein. However, in the way in which Quine's criticism was taken up and interpreted, there has been an omission of the first principle of the philosophy of language as it was expressed by Schlick, for example, in *"Die Wende der Philosophie"*:[5] philosophy is interested in meanings, or rather, in what we *mean*. From this point of view, Dummett's claim (in *Frege: Philosophy of Language*) that the primary goal of the philosophy of language is to analyze and understand meanings perhaps remains unshaken by decades of calling meaning into question; it is perhaps even confirmed by the consequences this has had within the philosophy of language.[6] Certain current debates (on relativism and realism, for example) *don't mean anything*. There is thus now a temptation (this can be seen in Putnam) to go back to a more serene and factual reflection on meaning, on the signification of a word, a phrase, and so forth: to return to Austin's questions in "The Meaning of a Word,"[7] the most Wittgensteinian of his essays.

In any case, it is not surprising that if we go back a bit, as I have sought to do, we see that ordinary language philosophy and Viennese positivism, despite their differences, have at times been equally rejected by those who wish to construct a naturalist science of language. The idea heard frequently today, that it is necessary to "go beyond" the linguistic turn, with a "new" mentalist or cognitivist turn, has its source in Fodor and Katz's criticism of the philosophy of language in all its forms, a criticism they began to formulate in 1962.

In "What's Wrong with the Philosophy of Language?" (1962) and "The Relevance of Linguistics to Philosophy"[8] (1965), Katz and Fodor in effect rejected logical empiricism and ordinary language philosophy simultaneously, since, for different reasons, neither managed, or tried, to produce what they were looking for at the time: a systematic conceptualization of language that, by specifying universals or invariants of language, would make it possible to resolve certain philosophical problems. It is clear, however, that such systematization is not something that somehow "escaped" the Viennese or Oxford theoreticians; rather, it is exactly what they called into question. In ways that are of course very different, the two schools deny the possibility of establishing universals or invariants in natural language that would make it possible to somehow explain its functioning. In order to see the continuity that can thus be established between the philosophy of logical positivism and that of ordinary language, it is particularly illuminating to examine the method Waismann follows in *Logik,*

Sprache, Philosophie (which was translated bizarrely into English as *The Principles of Linguistic Philosophy*—a title that effaces this continuity). Quine was, as always, particularly lucid on the matter of this continuity. In "Five Milestones of Empiricism," he brings together the Vienna Circle and ordinary language philosophy in their shared attention to the meaning and meaningfulness of sentences rather than words. "The English philosophers of ordinary language have likewise directed their analyses to sentences rather than to words, in keeping with the example that was set by both the earlier and the later work of their mentor Wittgenstein."[9] The philosophy of language is interested in *meaningfulness*, mean-ing. Whether Carnap's or Austin's, this philosophy does not seek to establish a universal science of language that would lead us to discover, about or in language, something external to it: something that we don't know. For Carnap or Quine, the task is not to discover but to construct and invent; for Austin or Wittgenstein, everything is already there, and it remains for us to discover that we know it. Here lies a fundamental difficulty of the philosophy of language: the fact that our language (including philosophical) is always "unhappy" (the expression is Bouveresse's): "permanently haunted by a guilty conscience and a feeling of failure, never certain of its status and possibilities."[10] Unfortunately, investigation of this difficulty seems almost to have disappeared from the field of analytic philosophy today. And it would seem that perhaps analytic philosophy has also lost, along with this investigation, a part of its properly critical dimension, as certain of its recent developments would testify.

Above all, Fodor and Katz contested the idea (which is, however, also present in a certain form in Chomsky) that we—that is, each one of us, each speaker of language—already know all there is to know about language. This is a theme Cavell develops in *The Claim of Reason*, and it was central to his first writings on ordinary language philosophy. For Cavell, as for Austin, what is lacking in linguistics is not data but a kind of attention to the data (what he calls Austin's "ear," "pitch"). What is lacking is the capacity to know what to do with linguistics's data, its givens; with our usages, with *what we know*. We could say the same thing about this not knowing as Cavell says about psychology, and the two questions are connected. "Unlike other practices we call sciences, one sometimes feels that academic psychology tells us less than we already know. As though what stops it from being physics, or even economics, say, is not that it isn't as precise and predictive, but that it doesn't know how to use what we already know about its subjects. One of the beauties of the practice of linguistics is that it gives, or ought to give, full play to our everyday knowledge of its data."[11]

Upon reflection, it is not really astonishing that from his earliest articles onward, Cavell was violently rejected by the partisans of a "real" science of language who, in the following years, turned, quite logically, to a cognitivist understanding of linguistic functioning. In "The Availability of What We Say" (1963; a title that combines and parodies two of these important first articles of Cavell's, "Must We Mean What We Say?" and "The Availability of Wittgenstein's Later Philosophy") and in the introduction to their book *The Structure of Language* (1964), Fodor and Katz criticized the idea—whose central role in ordinary language philosophy Cavell determined—that "I" know what "we" say and am capable of detecting an incorrect or bizarre expression, without any recourse to intuition or to a possible explanation by psychology.[12] Of course, from the beginning, Cavell pointed out the problematic nature of such a claim inherent in language use, but Katz and Fodor curiously reproached him for basing himself on linguistic intuition. But Cavell, like Austin, never maintained that we have a sort of innate or irrational intuition of what must be said. What interests him, and what he discovers in Austin and then more profoundly in Wittgenstein, is the problematic nature of our relationship to language and of my position as a *subject* of common language—a position that can be explained neither in terms of psychology nor in terms of intersubjectivity, but irreducibly, as a claim.

This debate from the sixties is particularly representative of a permanent conflict over the status of the philosophy of language, a conflict that can be found in various forms throughout twentieth-century analytic philosophy, on account of the refusal of those who represent what must be called a "hard" or naturalist version of the philosophy of language to reflect on the everydayness, the ordinariness—the naturalness, in the sense of "natural" that I have tried to explain—of the linguistic given. The refusal of ordinary language philosophy, even (especially) when this refusal takes the form of a turn, or return, toward the philosophy of mind, is always a symptom: "ignorance of oneself is a refusal to know."[13] Cavell's perception back in the sixties was accurate: what is refused is, in a sense, language itself insofar as it is part of the given, insofar as it is our form of life (and thus, is us, Cavell would say).

It is also just as normal and natural that today's descendants of Katz and Fodor's positions in the sixties (including Fodor himself) advocate a new turn (having in fact been obliged to give up on the project of a universal science of language): a cognitivist turn, following the linguistic turn. But it seems to me that this is not so much a second, new turn as it is an emptying out of the first: ultimately the most interesting and radical problem raised by the linguistic turn is the idea that ordinary language already gives us everything there is to know and that there is nothing more. The refusal or repression of this idea is, for Cavell, inherent to the very constitution of the American analytic philosophy whose history I have tried to sketch. For Cavell, this is a repression that reiterates the repression of the first American philosophy, the transcendentalism of Emerson and Thoreau; but above all, the attitude of refusal reveals a more general unawareness, and a rejection of the ordinary by philosophy: "When I ask whether we may not see [Emerson and Thoreau] as part of our inheritance as philosophers, I am suggesting that our foreignness as philosophers to these writers . . . may itself be a sign of an impoverished idea of philosophy, of a remoteness from philosophy's origins, from what is native to it."[14]

The difficulty of knowing what must be *inherited* in philosophy, a constant theme of Cavell's, is inseparable from all work in philosophy—especially in the philosophy of language, where it is precisely a matter of determining what is "native" or natural to us and how this natural is always inherited, again and again. I am far from suggesting that some primary or purified origin of philosophy must be found. What is native to philosophy is precisely the question that I can ask, here and now, of what I know or want to know. In this sense, the famous answer "I know that I do not know" is *not* skeptical. It means: it is necessary to want to know.

> What I take Socrates to have seen is that, about the questions which were causing him wonder and hope and confusion and pain, he knew that he did not know what no man can know, and that any man could learn what he wanted to learn. No man is in any better position for knowing it than any other man—unless *wanting* to know is a special position. And this discovery about himself is the same as the discovery of philosophy, when it is the effort to find answers, and permit questions, which nobody knows the way to nor the answer to any better than you yourself.[15]

If we have learned anything from this journey through the philosophy of language, it is perhaps this: what counts is wanting to know. Here again it is a matter of learning. But to find one's way (one's voice) in philosophy—including in analytic philosophy—is not easy, for the will to know and confidence in oneself ("Self Reliance")—are sometimes suffocated by the accumulation of arguments and the conformity of doctrines. The directions I have sketched out here are ways of resisting certain dogmas of analytic philosophy, notably in its recent mentalist or scientist version—not by fleeing to the postanalytic, but, to the contrary, by returning to the beginnings of analytic philosophy, and not out of useless nostalgia, but in order to understand, simply, what was radical and fascinating, as well as *revolutionary*, in this philosophy. This goal is what led me to Austin and Wittgenstein as well as "back home" to Frege, Schlick, and Carnap. Several current versions of analytic philosophy—the philosophy of mind as it has been reconceived under the influence of the cognitive sciences, the scholasticism of moral philosophy, and neometaphysics, for example—often seem, in spite of the inventiveness and talent of their best American representatives, to have lost the critical radicalness that was at the source of contemporary discussions of language: a radicalness always present in the great analytic philosophers, including Quine and Davidson. It is in *critique* that their arguments—the thesis of the indeterminacy of translation, the critique of analyticity, the critique of the idea of a conceptual scheme—take on their philosophical importance and strike not just a whole section of logical positivism, as people sometimes content themselves with saying, but also the more recent certitudes of contemporary naturalism. And the central problem facing analytic philosophy today does indeed lie in defining naturalism. Naturalism, which had its source in Hume but often has Kantian echoes, has split into two directions. One naturalism consists in grounding science in nothing other than itself, without any first philosophy; it has produced some perverse effects and has led, as we have seen, either to relativism or to dogmatic realism. There is also what must be termed a second naturalism, which grounds our knowledge of the world in the immanence of our form of life and our uses of language. It is remarkable that these two versions of naturalism took shape and blended together in Quine: the naturalized epistemology version (immanent to science itself) and the anthropological version, the indeterminacy of radical translation. It is equally remarkable that these two naturalisms today seem to have become incompatible and trace two radically different interpretations of the problem of realism and the possibility and necessity for language to speak the real. It is not that the anthropo-logical point of view leads to renouncing thinking the relation of language to the world—but that the relation must henceforth be thought differently, and not within an epistemology condemned to scientism or relativism: it must be thought within the very nature of language, and in our own nature as speaking subjects. That is: in ordinary language, conceived of as the repository of what we *understand* by "real."

However, as we have seen, in relocating the problem of knowledge onto such anthropological ground, it is not a question of taking any common sense or "our" uses of language as primary ground—in spite of Austin's affirmations that if ordinary language is not the last word, it is at least "the first word." The reflection on ordinary language wishes precisely to come *after*, and it does not claim to offer a first philosophy, or anything primary whatsoever. It is carried out, on the contrary, within an acknowledgment of the fact that we do not immediately know what *our* uses of language are, that *our* agreements are not immediate or transparent at all, and that they must always be established: we do not know who this *we* is.

It is no longer only a matter of a discovery or construction (*Aufbau*) of the world, but of recognizing and claiming my voice in this world. Our agreements *in* language are not a priori or certain; they are fragile, and we ourselves do not know them well. It is not easy to know "what we mean" or "to mean" what we say, and this is an essential element of the thought of ordinary language, which is traversed by doubt, not about the possibility of saying but of *meaning to say*. Thus, skepticism is the symptom of the ever-present possibility of a break in the linguistic contract, of a loss of contact with language and hence with the world. The problem of realism turns out, definitively, to be less the (epistemological) problem of being able to suppose or posit the real than the (everyday) problem of being able to accept it, and to accept *being of it*. In this way, reflection on ordinary language leads to a definition of our ordinariness, conceived as our submission to the necessity and arbitrariness of language—submission to our *nature*, as Emerson says, as "victims of expression."[16]

It seems we are far from our first definitions of naturalism. But it is nevertheless still the same problem of the philosophy of knowledge as the one already raised by Kant on the basis of Hume: the problem of how it is possible for man to speak the world of which (with his language and science) he is part, to find his *voice* in the world he describes. The only way to adopt or at least to define a "realist" position, if that can still make any sense, would be to arrive at thinking the circularity and radical immanence that Quine recognized ("the truth is immanent"), without renouncing thinking the nature of language, the nature of usages and of our agreements. To do so would be to reinvent, as McDowell proposed in *Mind and World*, a naturalism of "second nature," against "bald naturalism," which leads fatally to a "myth of the given," to relativism, or to metaphysics.[17]

The "nature" of what in a sense is a renewed language—our nature as speakers, speaking subjects—is to speak the real and to have to "bear" speaking it, as it were. What is at stake then in *our* language is the (re)cognition, within it, of *my* proximity to the world; that is, of the *ordinary*, not metaphysical, fact that (to go back to Austin's declaration) "there must be something other than the words, which the words are to be used to communicate about: this may be called the 'world.' "[18] This is a fact of nature that can be neither spoken nor known (but is neither unsayable nor unknowable in the traditional sense of these terms)—it can only be *accepted*, "given," like Wittgenstein's "forms of life."

We are far from a transcendental argument here, as well as from any salvaging of truth by science; if there is a way to define an "immanent truth," it is precisely in the real immanence of ordinary language, its usages, its successes and failures: what I have attempted to define as its "appropriateness" or "adequacy"—not in any reference to our "conceptual scheme," to our cognitive capacities, or to the exploits of our perception. Thus, in the end, the aporias of realism and its relativist double dissolve, as does the myth of a return to apophantic transparency. The Kantian question of the foundation of knowledge, of an answer to skepticism, turns out to be the question of discovering and claiming my voice as a "universal voice," as Emerson's "Self Reliance" affirms, echoing the *Third Critique*: "To believe your own thought, to believe that what is true for you in your private heart is true for all men,—that is genius. . . . For the inmost in due time becomes the outmost.[19]

Here lies a possible path to reinventing realism or, to go back to Cora Diamond's theme, a "realistic spirit"—on the condition of putting ordinary language philosophy, Wittgenstein's and Austin's, at the center of the project for a philosophy of language, although traditional and current interpretations would tend to marginalize and even definitively eliminate it. Doing so calls for a "nonconformist" reading of the history of the philosophy of language: it is not the history of natural progress from the establishment of logical positivism to the triumph of cognitive sciences but rather a history rich in reversals, critiques, and questionings, as well as in heritages both successful and ambiguous: Quine's inheritance of Duhem and Carnap; Davidson, Rorty, and Putnam's of Quine; Cavell's of Emerson, Wittgenstein, and Austin—Cavell, who was a pioneer in maintaining analytic philosophy's need to go back to its history in order to "know itself." Such a nonconformist reading of history—as Emerson said in "Self-Reliance," self-reliance is the aversion of conformity[20]—would perhaps make it possible to imagine the question of realism (which is now overloaded to the point of scholasticism) differently. Without a doubt, this project of historical reinterpretation raises some difficulties with regard to the generally recognized cleavage between the "analytic" and "Continental" traditions. The fact is that beyond the conventional discourse on their rivalry or reconciliation, it is time, as Cavell says, to think *within* this fracture, to attempt to understand the reasons for it, instead of trying to reduce it; this is a project to which an examination of analytic philosophy as such could contribute. Such a reflection would make it possible to begin to rethink the nature of contemporary philosophy: instead of conceiving of it as simply divided between two rival poles, American and European, analytic and Continental, one of which is always seeking to dominate the other, one could go back to its history and rethink its various heritages: for example, the inheritance of Kant by Emerson before Nietzsche's inheritance of Emerson; and, in an apparently entirely different vein—but we have been able to see the relation between the two—the inheritance of Kant by Austro-German logical positivism that was soon imported to the United States. In this way, there is a double Kantian filiation that developed the problem of knowledge as it was raised in the *Critiques* along contradictory and complementary lines. It is indeed the Kantian problematic of knowledge and knowledge's limits that is taken up in Wittgenstein's *Tractatus* and in all of the Vienna Circle's philosophy, and it was later radicalized by Quine, Davidson, and Putnam. On the basis of this very problematic, however, another direction was also taken, initiated by Wittgenstein, Austin, and then Cavell: the discovery of my ordinary *voice* in the world, and acceptance, rather than demonstration, of the world's existence and my existence in it. It is clear, finally, that within this problematic relation to Kant—it is no longer a matter of "returning" to him, but of continuing to *respond* to him—are included certain of the most stimulating and original philosophical approaches in the analytic field today. I am thinking here of Diamond, McDowell, Conant, and others, who want to rethink "the mind" and "realism" in terms other than those of the so-called philosophy of mind.

It will be said that these are old problems and that the progress of the cognitive sciences in general and cognitive philosophy in particular have already gone beyond them—but nothing is less certain. First, because as Wittgenstein noted, progress in philosophy is never as great as one thinks, and second, because it is perhaps only by going back to the origins of the project of the philosophy of language that one may perceive what was *revolutionary* about it, to use a term shared by Cavell and Kuhn in the 1960s—the revolutionary being the one who brings change about from within (a science, a practice). Wittgenstein and Austin want to change how philosophers proceed, not in order to reject the past once more (that would be, as Putnam reminds us, to throw the baby out with the bath water),[21] but in order to restore meaning to their practice. "Only a master of the science can accept a revolutionary change as a natural extension of that science; and . . . he accepts it, or proposes it, in order to maintain touch with the idea of that science, with its internal canons of comprehensibility and comprehensiveness.[22]

In this reading (which is certainly not the standard reading of Kuhn, and which would be rejected both by those who admire him for what they claim to be his relativism and by those who see a serious threat to scientific rationality in his arguments), a revolution is a change in "natural reactions," via the development of a "new (human) nature."[23] The demand for change that can be read in Wittgenstein and in Austin is thus revolutionary—it is a call for change in our natural reactions, in our procedures, which would be immediately applicable and a source of education. "Because such writing as Wittgenstein's and such practice as Austin's strike certain minds as conservative . . . it is worth noting that these teachers thought of their work as revolutionary—not merely because what they did was new . . . but because they also thought it plain enough and immediately fruitful enough to establish a new common practice in thinking, and open to talent regardless of its standing within the old intellectual orders."[24]

The education (philosophy as "education of grownups") contributed by Austin and Wittgenstein bears on philosophy's claim—defined by Kant, and which Cavell also names "arrogation"—to speak in the name of others; we have seen how natural, and yet threatened by the very idea of ordinary language, this claim is. The philosophical refusal of the ordinary, and more specifically, the refusal, shared by analytic and Continental philosophy, of the procedures of ordinary language philosophy is a symptom of this fragility. "Perhaps the reason . . . is that philosophers have become threatened by an idea that philosophy has its limitations or impotencies."[25]

But the very status of the philosophical word is called into question by the thought of ordinary language. The philosopher speaks with ordinary words, and nothing says these words will be accepted by other humans, although the philosopher claims to speak for all.

Who is to say whether a man speaks for all men?

Why are we so bullied by such a question? Do we imagine that if it has a sound answer the answer must be obvious or immediate? But it is no easier to say who speaks for all men that it is to speak for all men.[26]

This shows that the question of the philosophical word—its specific arrogation—is the question of language itself: it touches on the refusal of language's *publicness*, which we so easily hide under a mythology of privacy. Isn't this last temptation inherent to philosophical discourse, despite (even *in*) its classic and more recent claims to be public, claims to clarity and "realism"? *To recover language*, and the real along with it: this is what is at stake in the thought of the ordinary and in the philosophical revolution that this thought aspires to, which undoubtedly still lies before us.

Notes

Preface

1. Stanley Cavell, "Declining Decline," in *This New Yet Unapproachable America*, 70.
2. Cited in Waismann, *Wittgenstein*, 142.
3. See my work *Penser l'ordinaire*.
4. Austin, *Sense and Sensibilia*, 3–4.
5. Wittgenstein, *Philosophical Investigations*, §107, p. 46.

Introduction

1. Published as Beck and Wahl, *La philosophie analytique*.
2. See Creath, *Dear Carnap, Dear Van*.
3. In Quine, *Logical Point of View*.
4. Laugier, *L'anthropologie logique*.
5. Austin, *Philosophical Papers*, 182.
6. Rorty, *Linguistic Turn*, 31.
7. See Hacking, *Why Does Language Matter?*
8. Chappell, *Ordinary Language*, 1.
9. Bouveresse, *La demande philosophique*, 12. [Translation mine.—Trans.]
10. Quine, "Discussion Générale," in Beck and Wahl, *La philosophie analytique*, 343. [Translation mine.—Trans.]
11. Ibid. [Translation mine.—Trans.]
12. I deal with this the first part of *L'anthropologie logique*.
13. Wittgenstein, *Philosophical Investigations*, §1, p. 2; Quine, *Word and Object*, ix.
14. Quine, "Natural Kinds," in *Ontological Relativity*, 128.

15. Quine, "Le mythe de la signification," 139–70.

16. Hilary Putnam, *The Threefold Cord* (New York: Columbia University Press, 2001).

17. Waismann, *Principles of Linguistic Philosophy.*

18. Rorty, *Linguistic Turn*, 12.

19. Wittgenstein, *Tractatus Logico-Philosophicus*, 6.54, p. 108.

20. J. L. Austin, "A Plea for Excuses," in *Philosophical Papers*, 175–204.

21. Wittgenstein, *Philosophical Investigations*, §108, p. 46.

22. Wittgenstein, *Foundations of Mathematics*, 325.

23. Wittgenstein, *Tractatus Logico-Philosophicus*, 5.641, p. 72.

24. See my synthesis, "Y a-t-il une philosophie?"

Chapter One

1. It is well known especially since Jacques Bouveresse's analysis in *La parole malheureuse.*

2. The fourth Colloque de Royaumont in 1958 brought together Anglo-Saxon and French philosophers, and the talks given there were published in French as Beck and Wahl, *La philosophie analytique.*

3. Quine, "Le mythe de la signification," 139. [Translation mine.—Trans.]

4. See my article "Frege et le mythe de la signification."

5. Quine, *Logical Point of View*, 48.

6. Quine, "Ontological Relativity," in *Ontological Relativity*, 27.

7. Quine, "Facts of the Matter," 166–67.

8. Quine, *Theories and Things*, 46–47.

9. Wittgenstein, *Philosophical Investigations*, §547, pp. 146–47.

10. Quine, "Le mythe de la signification," 139. [Translation mine.—Trans.]

11. Quine, *Theories and Things*, 45.

12. The expression appears for the first time in *Theories and Things.*

13. Wittgenstein, *Foundations of Mathematics*, 325.

14. Quine, "Is Logic a Matter of Words?"

15. Ibid.

16. Cavell, *Claim of Reason*, 86–125.

17. Skorupski, "Empiricism, Verification, and the *a priori*," 158.

18. Donald Davidson, "On the Very Idea of a Conceptual Scheme" (1974), re-published in *Inquiries into Truth*, 183–98.

19. Quine, *Logical Point of View*, 43.

20. See my article "Une ou deux indéterminations."

21. See, for example, the chapter "A Comparison of Something and Something Else," in Putnam, *Words and Life*, 330–50.

Chapter Two

1. See Laugier, "Une ou deux indéterminations."
2. Quine, *Logical Point of View*, 44.
3. Davidson, *Inquiries into Truth*, 198.
4. In addition to Geertz's essay "Anti Anti-Relativism," see Laugier, "Relativité linguistique."
5. Putnam, *Words and Life*, 287.
6. Davidson, *Inquiries into Truth*, 198.
7. Quine, *Logical Point of View*, 103.
8. Harman, "Quine on Meaning and Existence," 346.
9. Quine, *Logical Point of View*, 103.
10. Quine, "Discussion Générale," in Beck and Wahl, *La philosophie analytique*, 343. [Translation mine.—Trans.]
11. Quine, *Roots of Reference*, 88.
12. Quine, *Theories and Things*, 20.
13. Quine, *Roots of Reference*, 88.
14. Quine, *Ontological Relativity*, 53.
15. Quine, *Theories and Things*, 23.
16. Donald Davidson, "A Nice Derangement of Epitaphs," in LePore, *Truth and Interpretation*, 446.
17. Cited in Rorty, *Linguistic Turn*, 373.

Chapter Three

1. Quine, *Ontological Relativity*, 49.
2. Ibid., 25.
3. Quine, *Word and Object*, 24–25.
4. Paul Gochet, in Meyer, *La philosophie anglosaxonne*, 343.
5. Quine, *Theories and Things*, 21.
6. Ibid.
7. Ibid., 22.
8. Quine, *Philosophy of Logic*, 12.
9. Ibid., 11, 97.
10. J. L. Austin, "Truth," in *Philosophical Papers*, 117.
11. Quine, *Philosophy of Logic*, 11.
12. Austin, *Philosophical Papers*, 117.
13. Quine, "Symposium on Austin's Method," in Fann, *Symposium on J. L. Austin*, reprinted in Quine, *Theories and Things*.
14. Austin, *Philosophical Papers*, 133.

15. Ibid., 118.

16. See my article "Dire et vouloir dire."

17. See the collection *Truth*, edited by Pitcher, which includes the important texts of the debate. The discussion has recently been taken up by Searle, who also defends Austin against Strawson, for reasons quite different from mine here.

18. He rejects correspondence in the article "Truth," in *Philosophical Papers*, 124–26.

19. Ibid., 125.

Chapter Four

1. In the important "Dewey Lectures": Hilary Putnam, "Sense, Nonsense, and the Senses: An Inquiry into the Powers of the Human Mind," in *The Threefold Cord* (New York: Columbia University Press, 2001), 10.

2. See Bouveresse, *Langage, perception, et réalité*.

3. Fann, *Symposium on J. L. Austin*.

4. This is exactly the expression Austin uses in "Truth," as Quine noted in his commentary.

5. Quine, *Philosophy of Logic*, 1.

6. Frege, "Thought," 307.

7. In Quine, *Ways of Paradox*, 265–71.

8. Quine, *Philosophy of Logic*, 2.

9. Quine, "Review of *An Inquiry into Truth and Meaning*," 29–30.

10. Quine, *Theories and Things*, 82–83.

11. Carnap, *Meaning and Necessity*, 215.

12. Quine, *Logical Point of View*, 41.

13. Duhem, *Aim and Structure*, 159.

14. Thomas Kuhn, "Reflections on My Critics," in Lakatos and Musgrave, *Criticism and the Growth of Knowledge*, 267.

15. Karl Popper, "Normal Science and Its Dangers," in Lakatos and Musgrave, *Criticism and the Growth of Knowledge*, 51–58.

16. Kuhn, "Reflections on My Critics," 267.

17. In Rorty, Schneewind, and Skinner, *Philosophy in History*.

18. Quine, *Word and Object*, 3.

19. See Duhem, *Aim and Structure*, 150.

20. Quine, *Philosophy of Logic*, 100.

21. Kuhn, "Reflections on My Critics," 231–78. See also Laugier, "Relativité linguistique," 47–73.

22. Quine develops this argument especially in *Theories and Things* and *Pursuit of Truth*.

23. Ian Hacking, *Representing and Intervening: Introductory Topics in the Philosophy of Natural Science* (Cambridge: Cambridge University Press, 1983).

24. Putnam, "Models and Reality," 421–45.

25. See Searle, *Construction of Social Reality*, in particular chaps. 6 and 8.

26. See Laugier, *L'anthropologie logique*, part 1, chap. 3, and part 2, chap. 3.

27. Quine, *Ontological Relativity*, 28.

28. Austin, *Philosophical Papers*, 154.

29. Ibid., 122.

30. Strawson, *Logico-Linguistic Papers*, 153n1.

31. I cannot understand why Austin's great article "Unfair to Facts" disappeared from the French translation of his *Philosophical Papers*.

32. Conant, "Method of the *Tractatus*," 374–462.

33. Wittgenstein, *Philosophical Investigations*, §108.

34. Austin, *Philosophical Papers*, 125.

35. See Diamond, *Realistic Spirit*, introductions 1 and 2, chaps. 2, 3, 5.

36. Let us note here a translation error in the French edition, *Ecrits philosophiques*, 100, where "truly" is translated as "sincerely," which makes Austin's entire philosophical point in "Truth" disappear.

37. Austin, *Philosophical Papers*, 124.

38. Ibid.

39. Ibid., 158.

40. For example, Peter Strawson imagines that Austin does not know the difference between a thing and a fact. See Pitcher, *Truth*, 35–118.

41. Austin, *Philosophical Papers*, 158–59.

42. Strawson, *Logico-Linguistic Papers*, 147.

43. Davidson takes up the idea of a purified or improved theory of correspondence at the end of his article "True to the Facts." See *Inquiries into Truth*, 54.

Chapter Five

1. Austin, *Philosophical Papers*, 124.

2. "One can't abuse ordinary language without paying for it." Austin, *Sense and Sensibilia*, 15.

3. See Bouveresse, *Langage, perception, et réalité*.

4. Austin, *Sense and Sensibilia*, 3.

5. See Marr, *Vision*, 31.

6. Bouveresse, *Langage, perception, et réalité*, 206.

7. Austin, *Sense and Sensibilia*, 4.

8. Wittgenstein, *Philosophical Investigations*, §308, p. 103.

9. For a more detailed analysis, see my article "Dire et vouloir dire."

10. Austin, "Other Minds," in *Philosophical Papers*, 87–88.

11. See Cavell, *Claim of Reason*, chaps. 3–4.

12. Austin, *Philosophical Papers*, 90.

13. Quine, *Theories and Things*, 40.

14. Austin, *Sense and Sensibilia*, 11.

15. Ibid., 9.

16. Here, Quine's skepticism would be welcome.

17. Austin, *Sense and Sensibilia*, 9.

18. Descombes, *Mind's Provisions*, 74 (*La denrée mentale* [Paris: Les Editions de Minuit, 1995]).

19. Austin, *Sense and Sensibilia*, 10.

20. Ibid., 11.

21. Austin, *Philosophical Papers*, 55–75.

22. Austin, *Sense and Sensibilia*, 11.

23. Ibid.

24. For Austin the famous example of the broken stick is not at all an illusion. See *Sense and Sensibilia*, 30: all *that we see* is a stick dipped into water, and what would be bizarre would be if it were to appear otherwise (straight, for example) to us.

25. Austin, *Sense and Sensibilia*, chaps. 4, 5, 6.

26. Ibid., 99.

27. Ibid.

28. Ibid., 70.

29. Ibid., 64; see also 51.

30. Ibid., 51.

31. Bouveresse, *Langage, perception, et réalité*, 256–57.

32. Austin, *Sense and Sensibilia*, 62.

33. Austin, *Le langage de la perception*, 36.

34. Ibid., 7.

35. Austin, "Pretending," in *Philosophical Papers*, 271.

Chapter Six

1. Austin, "Truth," in *Philosophical Papers*, 121.

2. Quine, "Discussion générale," in Beck and Wahl, *La philosophie analytique*, 343. [Translation mine.—Trans.]

3. Austin, "Discussion générale," in Beck and Wahl, *La philosophie analytique*, 333–34. [Translation mine.—Trans.]

4. Austin, *Philosophical Papers*, 117. The translation of *size* as *mesure* (measure, dimension) in the French version seems excessively theoretical: it is indeed a matter of size in the ordinary, material sense.

5. Fann, *Symposium on J. L. Austin*, 83.

6. Ibid.

7. Austin, *Sense and Sensibilia*, 5. Note the allusion to Jane Austen's *Sense and Sensibility* with the use of the adjective "sensible."

8. Austin, "Discussion générale," in Beck and Wahl, *La philosophie analytique*, 334. [Translation mine.—Trans.]

9. Ibid., 334. [Translation mine.—Trans.]

10. Ibid., 334–35. [Translation mine.—Trans.]

11. Austin, *Philosophical Papers*, 183.

12. Ibid., 185.

13. Ibid., 182.

14. Ibid.

15. Cavell, *Must We Mean What We Say?* 102–3.

16. Ibid., 100.

17. Austin, *Philosophical Papers*, 181.

18. See Ryle, "Ordinary Language," 29–31.

19. ["A usage is a custom, practice, fashion or vogue. It can be local or widespread, obsolete or current, rural or urban, vulgar or academic. There cannot be a misusage any more than there can be a miscustom or a misvogue." Ibid., 31.—Trans.]

20. Austin, *Philosophical Papers*, 185.

21. Ibid., 274.

22. See Laugier, *L'anthropologie logique de Quine*, part 1; and, of course, Cavell, *Claim of Reason*.

23. Austin, *Philosophical Papers*, 182.

24. See Benoist, "Qu'est-ce qui est donné?"

25. See Bouveresse, *Langage, perception, et réalité*, in particular the introduction.

26. Quine, *Ontological Relativity*, 83.

27. Austin, *Philosophical Papers*, 77–116.

28. Austin, *Philosophical Papers*, 106–7, 130. Austin is not directly criticizing Hume here, but rather Wisdom in his much discussed book *Other Minds* (Oxford: Blackwell, 1952).

29. On this point, see Bouveresse's analysis of *On Certainty* in *Le mythe de l'intériorité*, chap. 5.

30. Austin, *Philosophical Papers*, 107.

31. Ibid., 97.

32. Austin, *Sense and Sensibilia*, 11.

33. See Marr, *Vision*; or the references to Austin in Casati and Dokic, *La philosophie du son*.

34. See Putnam, "Dewey Lectures."

35. See Cavell, *Pursuits of Happiness*.

36. Austin, *Philosophical Papers*, 130.

37. Austin, *How to Do Things with Words*, 144.

38. Wittgenstein, *Philosophical Investigations*, part 2, p. 215.

39. Ibid.

40. Austin, *How to Do Things with Words*, 145.

Chapter Seven

1. Published in Austin, *Philosophical Papers*, 55–75.

2. Austin, *Philosophical Papers*, 81.

3. Bouveresse, *Le mythe de l'intériorité*, 535–702; for the comparison with Austin, 600–603.

4. Austin, *Philosophical Papers*, 98–103, for the parallel between I know–I promise.

5. "Two Accounts of Knowing," in Friedrich Waismann, *Philosophical Papers*, 184.

6. Waismann, *Wille und Motiv*.

7. Cavell, *Claim of Reason*, 15.

8. Wittgenstein, *Blue and Brown Books*, 59.

9. Wittgenstein, *Philosophical Investigations*, §242.

10. Cavell, *Claim of Reason*, 118.

11. Wittgenstein, *Philosophical Investigations*, §32.

12. Wittgenstein, *Blue and Brown Books*, 31.

13. Quine, *Word and Object*, ix.

14. See my article "De Quine à Carnap," 541–55.

15. Fann, *Symposium on J. L. Austin*, 87.

16. Austin, *Philosophical Papers*, 55.

17. Cavell, *Must We Mean What We Say?* 52.

18. McDowell, "Virtue and Reason," 331–50, italics mine.

19. See my article "Communauté, tradition, réaction," 13–38.

Chapter Eight

1. Cavell, *Claim of Reason*, 20.

2. Ibid.

3. Ibid.

4. Cavell, *Senses of Walden*, 92–93.

5. Bouveresse, *Le mythe de l'intériorité*, chap. 5, para. 4, for example.

6. Norman Malcolm, "Moore and Ordinary Language," in Chappell, *Ordinary Language*, 6–7.

7. Cavell, *Claim of Reason*, 22.

8. Wittgenstein, *Philosophical Investigations*, §§241–42.

9. Cavell, *Claim of Reason*, 31.

10. Ibid., 123.

11. Cavell, *This New Yet Unapproachable America*, 42–45.

12. Wittgenstein, *Philosophical Investigations*, §107.

13. Cavell, *Must We Mean What We Say?* 42.

14. Cavell, *Claim of Reason*, 125.

15. Ibid.

16. Emerson, "Experience," in *Essays and Lectures*, 491.

17. Cavell, *This New Yet Unapproachable America*, 46.

18. Ibid., 81.

19. Wittgenstein, *Philosophical Investigations*, §90.

20. Cavell, *In Quest of the Ordinary*, 170.

21. Cavell, "Uncanniness of the Ordinary," 106.

22. Thoreau, *Walden*, 97, cited in Cavell, "Uncanniness of The Ordinary," 106.

23. Cavell, *In Quest of the Ordinary*, 4.

24. Cavell, *Claim of Reason*, 127; Kant, *Critique of Pure Reason*, 99.

25. Cavell, *Claim of Reason*, 18.

26. Ibid.

27. Cavell, "The Conversation of Justice," in *Conditions Handsome and Unhandsome*, 101.

28. Ibid., 32.

29. Cavell, *Must We Mean What We Say?* 86.

30. Ibid., 88.

31. Kant, *Critique of the Power of Judgment*, 99.

32. Ibid, 99.

33. Wittgenstein, *Philosophical Investigations*, §§241–42.

34. Cavell, *Must We Mean What We Say?* 94.

35. Ibid., 103.

36. Ibid., 96.

37. Montefiore and Williams, introduction to *British Analytical Philosophy*, 11. See also in the same volume Pears, "Austin and Wittgenstein."

Chapter Nine

1. See Pears, "Austin and Wittgenstein"; and Cavell, "Austin at Criticism," in *Must We Mean What We Say?*

2. With the notable exceptions today of Bouveresse, Putnam, and Diamond.

3. See MacIntyre, *After Virtue*.

4. Imbert, *Phénoménologies et langues formulaires*, 137.

5. Wittgenstein, *Tractatus Logico-Philosophicus*, 109, 53.

6. See Bouveresse, *Dire et ne rien dire*, chap. 7.

7. Diamond, *Realistic Spirit*, 2.

8. Wittgenstein, *Philosophical Investigations*, §500.

9. Diamond, *Realistic Spirit*, 2.

10. Geach, "Saying and Showing," is a foundational text.

11. Récanati, "Du positivisme logique."

12. Récanati, "Du positivisme logique." [Translation mine.—Trans.]

13. Cavell, *Themes out of School*, 36.

14. Diamond, *Realistic Spirit*, for example, chap. 6, "Throwing Away the Ladder."

15. Geach, "Saying and Showing," 56.

16. Ibid., 70.

17. Austin, *How to Do Things with Words*, 150.

18. See Fann, *Symposium on J. L. Austin*, 86.

19. Austin, *How to Do Things with Words*, 144.

20. Ibid., 148–49.

21. Ibid., 109.

22. Austin, *Philosophical Papers*, 133.

23. Ibid., 126.

24. Austin, *How to Do Things with Words*, 50.

25. Ibid., 52.

26. In Austin, *Philosophical Papers*, 175.

27. Cavell, *Pitch of Philosophy*, 87.

28. Ibid.

29. Austin, *Philosophical Papers*, 178.

30. In *Must We Mean What We Say*, 1.

31. Cavell, *Pitch of Philosophy*, 125.

32. Cavell, *Must We Mean What We Say?* 40.

33. Cavell, *Pitch of Philosophy*, 126.

34. Emerson, "Experience," in *Essays and Lectures*, 482.

35. Cavell, *Pitch of Philosophy*, 126.

36. Cavell, *Claim of Reason*, 351.

37. Ibid.

38. Ibid., 383.

39. See Wittgenstein, *Tractatus Logico-Philosophicus*, 5.641.

40. Wittgenstein, *Philosophical Investigations*, §§107–8.

41. Wittgenstein, *Philosophical Remarks*, §18.

42. Wittgenstein, *Philosophical Investigations*, §108.

43. Ibid., §454.

44. See Diamond, *Realistic Spirit*, 181, 194.

45. Kant, *Gesammelte Schriften*, 14.

46. Austin, "Translator's Preface," in Frege, *Foundations of Arithmetic*.

47. Wittgenstein, *Philosophical Investigations*, §241.

48. Ibid., §242.

Conclusion

1. Récanati, "Du positivisme logique."

2. Austin, *Philosophical Papers*, 232.

3. Wittgenstein, *Notebooks*, 44e, 1.5.15, 78.

4. Wittgenstein, *Zettel*, §712.

5. Schlick, *Philosophical Papers*, 2:154–60 and 2:157 in particular.

6. Dummett, *Frege*, 669.

7. In Austin, *Philosophical Papers*, 55.

8. Katz, "Relevance of Linguistics to Philosophy." Also published as "The Philosophical Relevance of Linguistic Theory" in Rorty, *Linguistic Turn*, 340–56.

9. Quine, *Theories and Things*, 70.

10. Bouveresse, *La parole malheureuse*, 11. [Translation mine.—Trans.]

11. Cavell, *Claim of Reason*, 93.

12. Introduction to Fodor and Katz, *Structure of Language*, 15–16.

13. Cavell, "The Availability of Wittgenstein's Later Philosophy," in *Must We Mean What We Say*, 72.

14. Cavell, *Senses of Walden*, 148.

15. Cavell, *Must We Mean What We Say*, foreword, xxviii.

16. Emerson, *Essays and Lectures*, 482.

17. McDowell, *Mind and World*, 83–85, 89–91.

18. Austin, *Philosophical Papers*, 121.

19. Emerson, "Self Reliance," in *Essays and Lectures*, 259.

20. Ibid., 261.

21. Putnam, "Dewey Lectures," 3.

22. Cavell, *Claim of Reason*, 121.

23. Ibid., 194.

24. Cavell, *Must We Mean What We Say?* xxv.

25. Ibid., xxvi.

26. Ibid.

Bibliography

Austin, John Langshaw. *Ecrits philosophiques*. Translated by Lou Aubert and Anne-Louise Hacker. Paris: Le Seuil, 1994.

———. *How to Do Things with Words*. New York: Clarendon Press, 1962.

———. *Le langage de la perception*. Translated by Paul Gochet. Paris: Armand Colin, 1971.

———. *Philosophical Papers*. Oxford, New York: Clarendon Press, 1961.

———. *Quand dire c'est faire*. Translated by G. Lane. Paris: Le Seuil, 1970. 2nd ed., with postface by François Récanati, Paris: Points-Seuil, 1991.

———. *Sense and Sensibilia*. Oxford: Oxford University Press, 1962.

Ayer, Alfred Jules, ed. *Logical Positivism*. New York: Free Press, 1959.

Beck, Leslie, and Jean Wahl, eds. *La philosophie analytique: Actes du 4ème colloque philosophique à Royaumont*. Cahiers du Royaumont. Paris: Minuit, 1962.

Benoist, Jocelyn. "Qu'est-ce qui est donné?" *Archives de Philosophie* 59, no. 4 (1996): 629–57.

Bouveresse, Jacques. *La demande philosophique*. Combas, France: L'éclat, 1996.

———. *Dire et ne rien dire*. Nimes, France: Editions J. Chambon, 1997.

———. *Langage, perception, et réalité*. Nimes, France: Editions J. Chambon, 1995.

———. *La parole malheureuse*. Paris: Editions de Minuit, 1971.

———. *Le mythe de l'intériorité*. Paris: Minuit, 1976.

Carnap, Rudolf. "The Elimination of Metaphysics through Logical Analysis of Language." In Ayer, *Logical Positivism*.

———. *The Logical Syntax of Language*. London: Routledge and Kegan Paul, 1937.

———. *Meaning and Necessity*. Chicago: University of Chicago Press, 1947.

Casati, Roberto, and Jérôme Dokic. *La philosophie du son*. Nimes, France: Editions J. Chambon, 1994.

Cavell, Stanley. "The Availability of Wittgenstein's Later Philosophy." *Philosophical Review* 71, no. 1 (January 1962): 67–93.

———. *The Claim of Reason*. New York: Oxford University Press, 1979.

———. *Conditions Handsome and Unhandsome: The Constitution of Emersonian Perfectionism*. Chicago: University of Chicago Press, 1991.

———. *In Quest of the Ordinary*. Chicago: University of Chicago Press, 1988.

———. "Must We Mean What We Say?" *Inquiry* 1, nos. 1–4 (1958): 172–212.

———. *Must We Mean What We Say?* 1969. Reprint, Cambridge: Cambridge University Press, 1976. Page citations are to the 1976 edition.

———. *A Pitch of Philosophy*. Cambridge, MA: Harvard University Press, 1994.

———. *Pursuits of Happiness*. Cambridge, MA: Harvard University Press, 1981.

———. *The Senses of Walden*. Expanded ed. Chicago: University of Chicago Press, 1992. First published in 1972.

———. *Themes out of School*. San Francisco: North Point Press, 1984.

———. *This New Yet Unapproachable America*. Albuquerque: Living Batch Press, 1989.

———. "The Uncanniness of the Ordinary." In *The Tanner Lectures on Human Values*, vol. 8. Cambridge: Cambridge University Press, 1989.

Chappell, Vere Claiborne. *Ordinary Language*. Englewood Cliffs, NJ: Prentice Hall, 1964.

Conant, James. "The Method of the *Tractatus*." In *From Frege to Wittgenstein: Perspectives on Early Analytic Philosophy*, edited by Erich Reck. Oxford: Oxford University Press, 2002.

Creath, Richard, ed. *Dear Carnap, Dear Van: The Quine-Carnap Correspondence and Related Work*. Berkeley: University of California Press, 1990.

Davidson, Donald. *Inquiries into Truth and Interpretation*. Oxford: Clarendon Press, 1984.

———. "On the Very Idea of a Conceptual Scheme." *Proceedings and Addresses of the American Philosophical Association* 47 (1973–74): 5–20.

Descombes, Vincent. *The Mind's Provisions: A Critique of Cognitivism*. Translated by Stephen Schwartz. Princeton, NJ: Princeton University Press, 2001.

Diamond, Cora. *The Realistic Spirit: Wittgenstein, Philosophy, and the Mind*. Cambridge, MA: MIT Press, 1995.

Duhem, Pierre. *The Aim and Structure of Physical Theory*. Princeton, NJ: Princeton University Press, 1954.

Dummett, Michael. *Frege: Philosophy of Language*. London: Duckworth, 1973.

Emerson, Ralph Waldo. *Essays and Lectures*. New York: Library of America, 1983.

Fann, K. T., ed. *Symposium on J. L. Austin*. London: Routledge and Kegan Paul, 1969.

Fodor, Jerry, and Jerold Katz. "The Availability of What We Say." *Philosophical Review* 72, no. 1 (January 1963): 57–71.

———. *The Structure of Language*. Englewood Cliffs, NJ: Prentice Hall, 1964.

———. "What's Wrong with the Philosophy of Language?" *Inquiry* 5, no. 1 (1962): 197–237.

Frege, Gottlob. *The Foundations of Arithmetic*. Translated by J. L. Austin. Oxford: Blackwell, 1953.

———. "Sense and Reference." *Philosophical Review* 57, no. 3 (May 1948): 209–30.

———. "The Thought: A Logical Inquiry." *Mind* 65, no. 259 (July 1956): 289–311.

Geach, Peter. "Saying and Showing in Frege and Wittgenstein." In Hintikka, *Acta philosophica Fennica*.

Geertz, Clifford. "Anti Anti-Relativism." *American Anthropologist* 86, no. 2 (June 1984): 263–78.

Hacking, Ian. *Why Does Language Matter to Philosophy?* Cambridge: Cambridge University Press, 1975.

Harman, Gilbert. "Quine on Meaning and Existence." *Review of Metaphysics* 21, no. 1 (1967): 124–51.

Hintikka, Jaako, ed. *Acta philosophica Fennica: Essays on Wittgenstein in the Honour of G. H. Von Wright*. Amsterdam: North Holland, 1976.

Imbert, Claude. *Phénoménologies et langues formulaires*. Paris: Presses Universitaires de France, 1992.

Katz, Jerold. "The Relevance of Linguistics to Philosophy." *Journal of Philosophy* 62, no. 20 (1965): 590–602.

Kant, Immanuel. *The Critique of Pure Reason*. Edited by Paul Guyer. Cambridge: Cambridge University Press, 1998.

———. *The Critique of the Power of Judgment*. Edited by Paul Guyer. New York: Cambridge University Press, 2000.

———. *Gesammelte Schriften*. Vol. 9, *Logic*. Edited by Preußischen Akademie der Wissenschaften. 29 vols. Berlin: Walter de Gruyter, 1912.

Lakatos, Imre, and Alan Musgrave, eds. *Criticism and the Growth of Knowledge*. Cambridge: Cambridge University Press, 1970.

Laugier, Sandra. "Communauté, tradition, reaction." *Critique* 610 (March 1998): 13–38.

———. "De Quine à Carnap." *Revue internationale de philosophie*, special Quine edition, 51, no. 202 (October–December 1997): 541–56.

———. "Dire et vouloir dire: Austin et la philosophie." *Critique* 51 (January–February 1995).

———. "Frege et le mythe de la signification." In *Phénoménologie et logique*, edited by J. F. Courtine. Paris: PENS, 1996.

———. *L'anthropologie logique de Quine*. Paris: Vrin, 1992.

———. *Penser l'ordinaire: Une autre philosophie américaine*. Paris: Presses Universitaires de France, 1999.

———. "Relativité linguistique, relativité anthropologique." *Histoire, épistémologie, langage* 2, no. 18 (November 1996): 45–73.

———. "Une ou deux indéterminations." *Archives de philosophie* 58, no. 1 (January–March 1995): 73–96.

———. "Y a-t-il une philosophie post-analytique?" *Esprit* (October 1995): 16–35.

LePore, Ernest, ed. *Truth and Interpretation*. Oxford: Blackwell, 1986.

MacDonald, Graham, and Crispin Wright, eds. *Fact, Science, and Morality*. Oxford: Blackwell, 1986.

MacIntyre, Alistair. *After Virtue*. Notre Dame, IN: Notre Dame Press, 1981.

Marr, David. *Vision*. New York: W. H. Freeman, 1982.

McDowell, John. *Mind and World*. Cambridge, MA: Harvard University Press, 1994.

———. "Virtue and Reason." *Monist* 62, no. 3 (1979): 331–50.

Meyer, Michel, ed. *La philosophie anglosaxonne*. Paris: P.U.F., 1994.

Montefiore, Alan, and Bernard Williams, eds. *British Analytical Philosophy*. London: Routledge and Kegan Paul, 1966.

Ogden, Charles Kay, and Ivor Armstrong Richards. *The Meaning of Meaning*. 1923. Reprint, New York: Harcourt, Brace, Jovanovich, 1989.

Pears, David. "Austin and Wittgenstein." In Montefiore and Williams, *British Analytical Philosophy*.

Pitcher, George, ed. *Truth*. Englewood Cliffs, NJ: Prentice Hall, 1964.

Putnam, Hilary. "Dewey Lectures." In *The Threefold Cord: Mind, Body, and World*. New York: Columbia University Press, 2001.

———. "Models and Reality" (1980). In *Philosophy of Mathematics: Selected Readings*, 2nd ed., edited by Paul Benacerraf and Hilary Putnam. Cambridge: Cambridge University Press, 1983.

———. "Sense, Nonsense, and the Senses: An Inquiry into the Powers of the Human Mind." *Journal of Philosophy* 91, no. 9 (September 1994): 445–517.

———. *Words and Life*. Edited by James Conant. Cambridge, MA: Harvard University Press, 1994.

Quine, Willard Van Orman. "Facts of the Matter." In *Essays on the Philosophy of W. V. Quine,* edited by Robert Shahad and Chris Swoyer. Norman: University of Oklahoma Press, 1979.

———. *From a Logical Point of View*. Cambridge, MA: Harvard University Press, 1961. First published in 1953.

———. "Is Logic a Matter of Words?" In "Abstracts of Papers to be Read at the Thirty-Seventh Annual Meeting of the Eastern Division of the American Philosophical Association." *Journal of Philosophy* 34, no. 25 (December 9, 1937): 674.

———. "Le mythe de la signification." In Beck and Wahl, *La philosophie analytique*.

———. *Ontological Relativity and Other Essays*. New York: Columbia University Press, 1969.

———. *Philosophy of Logic*. Cambridge, MA: Harvard University Press, 1970.

———. "Review of *An Inquiry into Meaning and Truth*." *Journal of Symbolic Logic* 6, no. 1 (March 1941): 29–30.

———. *The Roots of Reference*. LaSalle, IL: Open Court, 1974.

———. *Theories and Things*. Cambridge, MA: Belknap Press, 1981.

————. *The Ways of Paradox*. Cambridge, MA: Harvard University Press, 1976.

————. *Word and Object*. Cambridge, MA: MIT Press, 1960.

Récanati, François. "Du positivisme logique à la philosophie du langage ordinaire: Naissance de la pragmatique." Postface to Austin, *Quand dire c'est faire* (1991).

Rorty, Richard. *The Linguistic Turn*. Chicago: University of Chicago Press, 1992. First published in 1967.

Rorty, Richard, Jerome B. Schneewind, and Quentin Skinner, eds. *Philosophy in History*. Cambridge: Cambridge University Press, 1987.

Ryle, Gilbert. "Ordinary Language." In Chappell, *Ordinary Language*.

Schlick, Moritz. *Philosophical Papers*. Dordrecht: Reidel, 1979.

Searle, John. *The Construction of Social Reality*. New York: Free Press, 1994.

Skorupski, John. "Empiricism, Verification, and the *a priori*." In MacDonald and Wright *Fact, Science, and Morality*.

Strawson, Peter. *Logico-Linguistic Papers*. Burlington, VT: Ashgate, 1971.

————. "Truth." In Pitcher, *Truth*.

Thoreau, Henry David. *Walden*. Princeton, NJ: Princeton University Press, 1971.

Waismann, Friedrich. *Logik, Sprache, Philosophie*. Stuttgart, Germany: Reclam, 1976.

————. *Philosophical Papers*. Edited by Brian McGuinness. Boston: D. Reidel, 1977.

————. *The Principles of Linguistic Philosophy*. Edited by R. Harre. New York: St. Martin's Press, 1965.

————. *Wille und Motiv: Zwei Abhandlung über Ethik und Handlungstheorie*. Stuttgart, Germany: Reclam, 1983.

————. *Wittgenstein and the Vienna Circle*. Edited by Brian McGuinness. Oxford: Basil Blackwell, 1979.

Wittgenstein, Ludwig. *The Blue and Brown Books*. New York: Harper and Row, 1958.

————. *Notebooks, 1917–1918*. 2nd ed. Edited by G. E. M. Anscombe and G. H. von Wright. Chicago: University of Chicago Press, 1984.

————. *Philosophical Investigations*. Edited by G. E. M. Anscombe. Oxford: Blackwell, 1958.

————. *Philosophical Remarks*. Edited by Rush Rhees. Chicago: University of Chicago Press, 1980.

————. *Remarks on the Foundations of Mathematics*. Rev. ed. Edited by G. H. von Wright, Rush Rhees, and G. E. M. Anscombe. Cambridge, MA: MIT Press, 1983.

————. *Tractatus Logico-Philosophicus*. Translated by Charles Kay Ogden. New York: Cosimo Classics, 2007.

————. *Zettel*. Oxford: Blackwell, 1967.

Index